I Heart Oregon Seven Wonders

*Hikes at the Oregon Coast, Mount Hood,
Columbia River Gorge, Smith Rock, Painted Hills,
Crater Lake and the Wallowas*

BY LISA D. HOLMES

Cover and interior design by Lisa D. Holmes (Yulan Studio, yulanstudio.com)

All photographs, maps and graphics are by the author, unless otherwise indicated.

Overview and section maps utilize terrain map data by OpenStreetMap, under CC-BY-SA.

Published in Portland, Oregon, by Yulan Studio, Inc.

Printed in the United States.

First edition

ISBN 978-0-9915382-4-9

SAFETY NOTICE

This book is intended as a resource to help plan a hike. Although every attempt has been made to provide accurate and current information on the hikes in this book, the publisher and the author are not responsible for any loss, damage or injury that may occur as a result of using this book – you hike at your own risk. Familiarize yourself with the area you intend to explore, check current weather reports, and check with regional recreation organizations listed in the Resource section of this book for more information on current conditions. You are responsible for your own safety and knowing your own limitations.

Contents

Contents *(continued)*

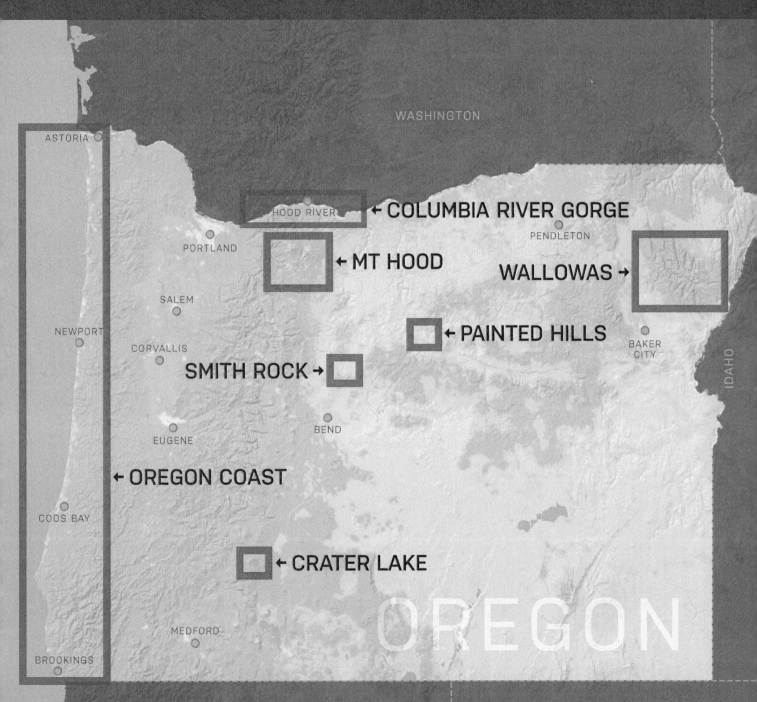

WASHINGTON

ASTORIA

HOOD RIVER ← **COLUMBIA RIVER GORGE**

PENDLETON

PORTLAND ← **MT HOOD**

WALLOWAS →

SALEM

NEWPORT

CORVALLIS

← **PAINTED HILLS**

BAKER
CITY

SMITH ROCK →

IDAHO

EUGENE

BEND

← **OREGON COAST**

COOS BAY

← **CRATER LAKE**

MEDFORD

OREGON

BROOKINGS

CALIFORNIA

NEVADA

Columbia
River
Gorge

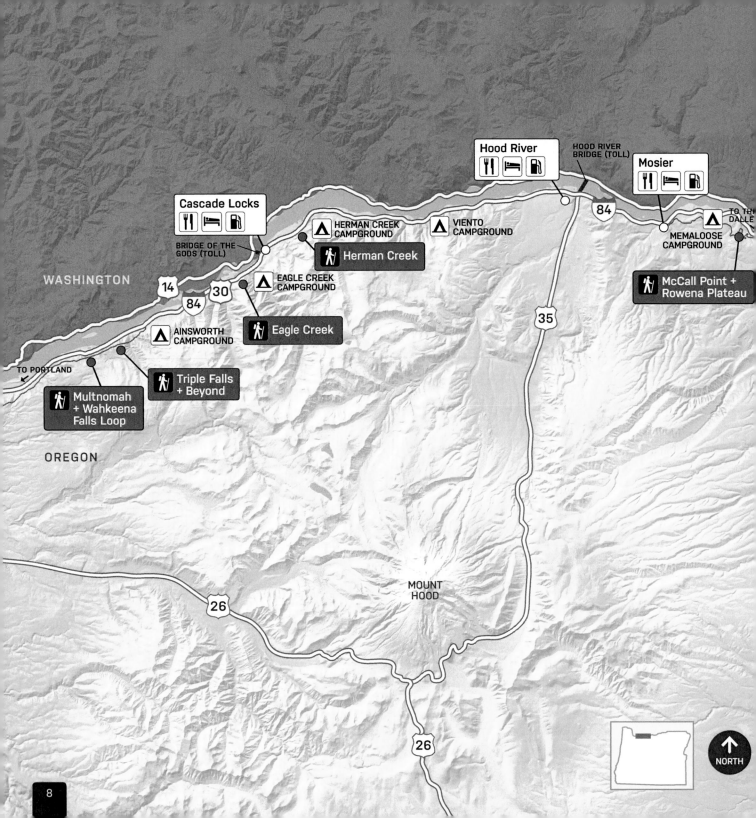

Hood River
🍴 🛏️ ⛽

HOOD RIVER
BRIDGE (TOLL)

Mosier
🍴 🛏️ ⛽

Cascade Locks
🍴 🛏️ ⛽

△ HERMAN CREEK
CAMPGROUND

△ VIENTO CAMPGROUND

84

BRIDGE OF THE
GODS (TOLL)

🥾 Herman Creek

△ MEMALOOSE
CAMPGROUND

TO THE
DALLES

△ EAGLE CREEK
CAMPGROUND

🥾 McCall Point +
Rowena Plateau

WASHINGTON

14

30

84

🥾 Eagle Creek

35

△ AINSWORTH
CAMPGROUND

TO PORTLAND

🥾 Triple Falls
+ Beyond

🥾 Multnomah
+ Wahkeena
Falls Loop

OREGON

26

MOUNT
HOOD

26

NORTH

The Columbia River cuts through the Cascade Mountain Range at sea-level, creating a gorge with cliffs up to 4,000 feet high.

Designated a National Scenic Area in 1986, the Columbia River Gorge is 85 miles long, from the Deschutes River near The Dalles to the Sandy River near Troutdale. Due to the extreme variability of elevation and precipitation, the Gorge is a place of incredible environmental diversity.

The western portion receives up to 100 inches of rain each year, creating temperate rain forests filled with streams and over 90 waterfalls. In Spring, the waterfalls are at their fullest, and the mossy forests are at their greenest, with woodland wildflowers alongside the trails.

The eastern side of the Gorge receives less than 15 inches of rain annually, rendering the landscape a virtual desert with rolling hills and rocky bluffs. Balsam root and lupine wildflowers fill the grasslands and meadows with bright colors in the spring.

A network of hiking trails running throughout the Gorge area range from easy and relatively flat (and family-friendly) to steep and extremely difficult. Most of the trails start near the river, climbing to ridges and viewpoints far above the river. The Gorge is also known as a leading center for windsurfing and kiteboarding due to a natural wind tunnel effect.

Metal bridge over Herman Creek (on the Herman Creek Bridge Trail); bridge above Triple Falls; Oneonta Creek footbridge.

Triple Falls & Beyond

Four waterfalls, a narrow slot canyon, viewpoints overlooking the Columbia River, two cascading creeks, plus moss and ferns covering everything in sight make this hike one of the best in the Columbia River Gorge.

Begin at the Horsetail trailhead, located directly next to Horsetail Falls (176 ft.). The first portion of the hike switchbacks up from the highway, gaining about 400 feet in 0.3 miles. After a section of mossy rock and views of the Columbia River, the trail heads inward to go behind Ponytail Falls (80 ft.), also known as Upper Horsetail Falls. The lava flow that created the falls covered soft soil, which over time has been washed away, creating the cavern behind the falls. From Ponytail Falls, continue another .25 miles to side trails that lead to great cliff-edge views of the Columbia River.

As the main trail begins a downward section of switchbacks, stop at a viewpoint looking down into the narrow 20 ft. wide slot canyon of Oneonta Gorge. Upon reaching the metal bridge over Oneonta Creek, Middle Oneonta Falls (24 ft.) is to the left. To the right, the creek drops off a ledge to unseen Lower Oneonta Falls (120 ft.). In late summer when water levels are at their lowest, it is possible to wade up the creek from the Oneonta trailhead to the base of this waterfall.

At the trail junction with Oneonta Trail 424, turn left to head to Triple Falls. (Shorter loop option: turn right to go back to the highway. This option results in a .25 mile walk along the road to return to the parking lot.) The trail to Triple Falls continues to gain elevation and is rocky and steep in a few spots. At Triple Falls (64 ft.), a side trail on the left leads to a closer view from a rocky slope directly across from the three-channel waterfall. The main trail continues on the right to a large wooden bridge that crosses the creek and enters a scenic area heavily covered with ferns, moss and lichens, making it look much like a fairyland. The trail is creekside for the next mile, with plenty of spots for observing or exploring alongside the creek.

After another mile, a small log bridge crosses the creek and everything becomes even more green than before. Continue to a trail junction and a clearing next to the creek for the final destination. Return the same way.

DISTANCE: 6.4 miles (roundtrip)

ELEVATION GAIN: 1,200 ft.

DIFFICULTY: moderate

HIKE TYPE: out and back

TRAIL: packed dirt and rock

OPEN: all year, but may be icy during the winter

BEST TIME OF YEAR: April - June and Oct. - Nov.

FEATURES: waterfalls, creeks, forest

FEES/PERMITS: none required

AGENCY: Columbia River Gorge National Scenic Area

DIRECTIONS TO TRAILHEAD

From Portland, take I-84 East for 25 miles to Bridal Veil Exit 28.

Turn right onto Bridal Veil Road.

A short distance ahead, turn left at the stop sign and intersection with the Historic Columbia River Hwy.

Drive 5.6 miles (2.5 miles past Multnomah Falls Lodge) to a small parking lot on the left, directly across from Horsetail Falls.

For an alternate route that bypasses the Multnomah Falls area, drive an additional 7 miles on I-84 and take the next exit, Ainsworth Exit 35. At the stop sign turn left (west) towards Multnomah Falls on the Historic Columbia River Hwy for 1.6 miles to the trailhead.

DRIVE TIME FROM PORTLAND
40 minutes

Photos, left to right from top: bridge above Triple Falls; mossy forest; Horsetail Falls; Oneonta Creek; footbridge.

TRIPLE FALLS + BEYOND

Photos, left to right from top: view of the Columbia River; grotto; bridge above Triple Falls; Oneonta Creek just before it falls into Oneonta Gorge; Ponytail Falls (Upper Horsetail Falls).

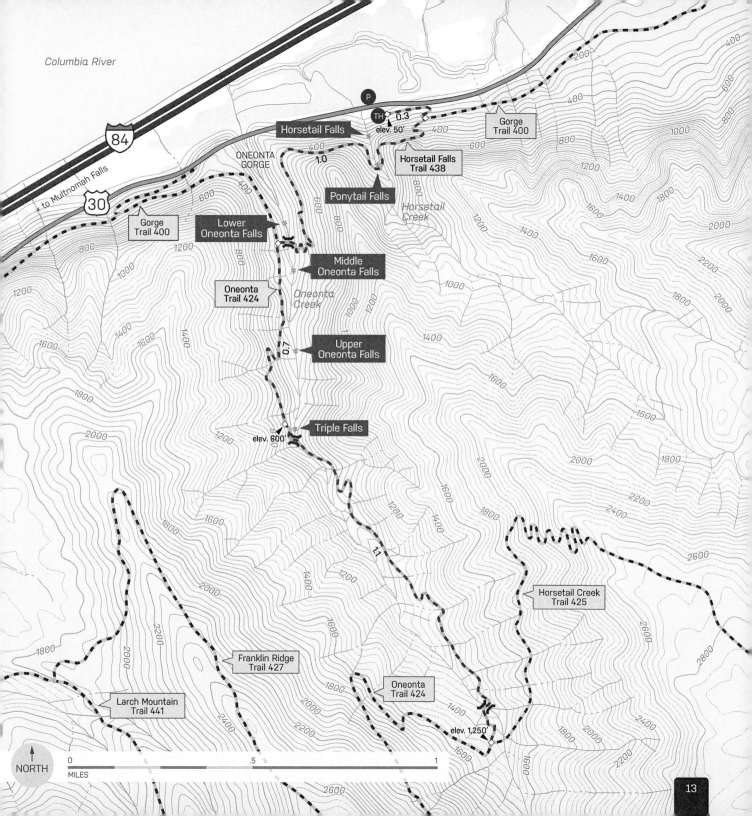

Columbia River

84

to Multnomah Falls

30

Gorge Trail 400

Horsetail Falls
TH 0.3
elev. 50'

P

ONEONTA GORGE

Horsetail Falls Trail 438

1.0

Ponytail Falls

Horsetail Creek

Lower Oneonta Falls

Gorge Trail 400

Middle Oneonta Falls

Oneonta Trail 424

Oneonta Creek

0.7

Upper Oneonta Falls

Triple Falls
elev. 600'

1.1

Horsetail Creek Trail 425

Franklin Ridge Trail 427

Oneonta Trail 424

elev. 1,250'

Larch Mountain Trail 441

NORTH

0   .5   1
MILES

13

Multnomah + Wahkeena Falls Loop

Six waterfalls, including Oregon's highest, two cascading spring-fed creeks meandering through lush greenery, and old-growth Douglas fir make this a spectacular loop hike.

Wahkeena is a Yakima Native American word meaning "most beautiful," which is quite appropriate for this creek and waterfall. Beginning at the Wahkeena Falls trailhead, cross the small stone bridge over the creek and begin a series of switchbacks on paved trail to a footbridge at the base of Wahkeena Falls (242 ft.). The height of the falls can seem deceptive because instead of falling in one plunge, it falls in a series of tiers, some of which are difficult to see from the trail. After several more switchbacks, you'll reach Lemmon's Viewpoint, with views of the Columbia River and across to Washington.

All along the uphill sections of trail, Wahkeena Creek rushes downhill, cascading through mossy rock next to ferns, berries and many wildflowers in the spring. One of the loveliest waterfalls along the hike, delicate Fairy Falls (20 ft.), cascades over a blocky basalt rock wall. To see the springs that appear from underground and are the source of Wahkeena Creek, turn right at the Angels Rest trail junction for about 100 yards. This is a scenic area, with the springs bubbling up from below ground, then pooling and meandering beneath large trees before heading downhill.

Return to the Wahkeena trail and head uphill, crossing a heavily wooded slope for about 1.5 miles before reaching the canyon of Multnomah Creek. The first waterfall along this section is Ecola Falls (55 ft.). Wiesendanger Falls (50 ft.) drops over a flat ledge of the creek into a rocky bowl. Just ahead on the trail is Dutchman's Tunnel, an overhang of basalt that creates a cave-like structure with tiny plants hanging down from the rock crevices. Dutchman Falls is a succession of three short falls along the creek just before a side trail to the overlook for Multnomah Falls.

A two-tiered waterfall, Multnomah Falls (620 ft.) is the highest waterfall in Oregon. With five different flows of lava visible in the rock face of Multnomah Falls, this is a good place to see evidence of the Gorge's geological history.

At the base of the falls is the historic Multnomah Lodge, built in 1915 around the same time as the Historic Columbia River Highway. Next to the lodge, take the roadside trail back to the Wahkeena Falls parking area.

DISTANCE: 5.4 miles (roundtrip)

ELEVATION GAIN: 1,600 ft.

DIFFICULTY: moderate

HIKE TYPE: loop

TRAIL: asphalt, packed dirt, rocks

OPEN: all year, but may be icy during the winter

BEST TIME OF YEAR: April - June and Oct. - Nov.

FEATURES: waterfalls, creeks, forest

FEES/PERMITS: none

AGENCY: Columbia River Gorge National Scenic Area

DIRECTIONS TO TRAILHEAD

From Portland, take I-84 East for 25 miles to Bridal Veil Exit 28.

Turn right onto Bridal Veil Road.

A short distance ahead, turn left at the stop sign and intersection with the Historic Columbia River Hwy.

Drive 2.5 miles to the parking lot for the Wahkeena Falls trailhead.

DRIVE TIME FROM PORTLAND
35 minutes

Photos, left to right from top: Multnomah Falls; Multnomah Creek; view of the Columbia River from Lemmon's Viewpoint; Multnomah Creek.

MULTNOMAH + WAHKEENA FALLS LOOP

Photos, left to right from top: Multnomah Creek; early fall forest; Wahkeena Spring; maidenhair ferns; Fairy Falls; side creek running into Multnomah Creek.

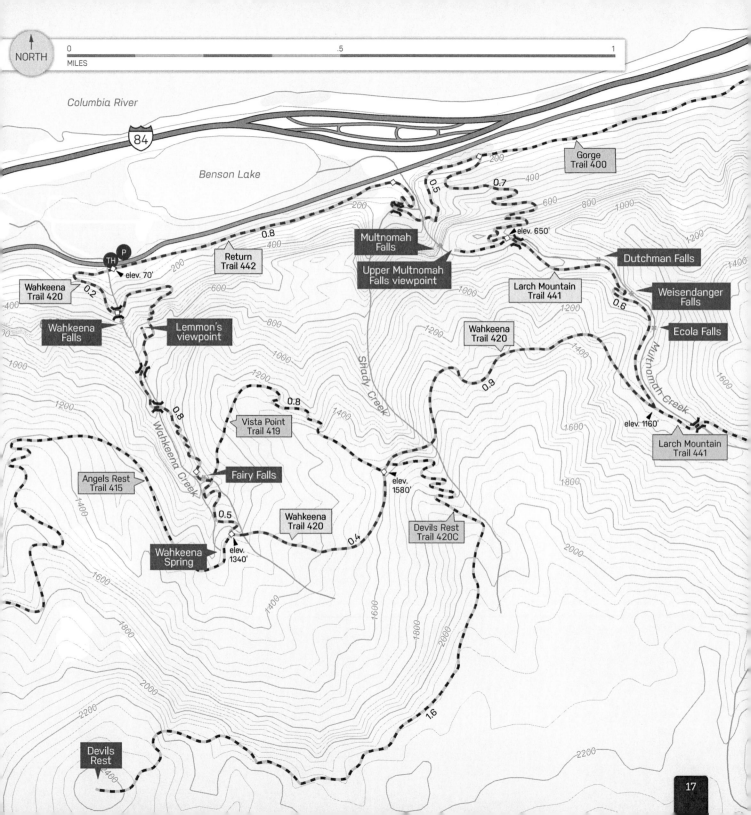

NORTH

0　　　　　　　　　　.5　　　　　　　　　　1
MILES

Columbia River

84

Benson Lake

Gorge
Trail 400

200

0.5

0.7

400

600

800

1000

1200

1400

elev. 650'

Dutchman Falls

Larch Mountain
Trail 441

Weisendanger
Falls

0.6

Ecola Falls

Multnomah Creek

0.8

400

Return
Trail 442

200

Multnomah Falls

Upper Multnomah
Falls viewpoint

elev. 70'

TH P

Wahkeena
Trail 420

0.2

Wahkeena
Falls

Lemmon's
viewpoint

600

800

1000

Shady Creek

1000

1200

1200

Wahkeena
Trail 420

0.9

1400

1600

elev. 1160'

Larch Mountain
Trail 441

0.8

Vista Point
Trail 419

1400

1200

Wahkeena Creek

0.8

Angels Rest
Trail 415

Fairy Falls

1400

elev.
1580'

1600

0.5

Wahkeena
Trail 420

0.4

Devils Rest
Trail 420C

Wahkeena
Spring

elev.
1340'

1400

1600

1800

2000

1600

2000

1800

1.6

2000

2200

1600

1800

2000

2200

Devils
Rest

1400

17

Eagle Creek to High Bridge

Along this three-mile stretch of the extremely popular Eagle Creek trail with its steep cliff walls, are three spectacular waterfalls, cascading side creeks, and a narrow slot canyon.

DISTANCE: 6.6 miles (roundtrip)

ELEVATION GAIN: 600 ft.

DIFFICULTY: easy to moderate

HIKE TYPE: out and back

TRAIL: packed dirt and rock

OPEN: all year, but may be icy during the winter

BEST TIME OF YEAR: April - June and Oct. - Nov.

FEATURES: waterfalls, forest, creek

FEES/PERMITS: none

AGENCY: Columbia River Gorge National Scenic Area

Built in 1915, the same year the Historic Columbia River Highway opened, the Eagle Creek trail is an engineering marvel. It was built using pick-axes and shovels, with sections of the trail blasted out of the vertical rock. The first several miles of trail have an easy grade with little elevation gain and plenty of spectacular scenery along the way.

The hike begins at the base of the Eagle Creek canyon with its towering basalt walls. The first section gently climbs through a forest of oak, big-leaf maple, cedar and Douglas fir before approaching the first of several sections of trail with steep drop-offs to the side and hand rails along the ledge. There is plenty of room on the trail, but it's easy for those afraid of heights to get a bit nervous, especially if you look down at the creek several hundred feet below.

At about one mile in, there's a short side trail to a viewpoint of Metlako Falls (82 ft.), which is named after the Native American goddess of salmon. After crossing a bridge with views of a scenic and mossy rock-lined side creek, a marked side trail for Punch Bowl Falls descends to an open rocky area along the creek beside Lower Punch Bowl Falls (12 ft.).

Just around the bend is the base of the famous Punch Bowl Falls (36 ft.) waterfall, plunging into its rocky circular bowl. Back on the main trail, just beyond the Punch Bowl side trail, is a view of this waterfall from high above, which makes for a good resting point. The next mile of trail crosses another small bridge over a lovely cascading side creek and passes through a large rockslide.

As the trail nears High Bridge, wispy two-tiered Loowit Falls (93 ft.) can be seen across a steep, narrow gorge. The first tier of Loowit Falls cascades about 90 feet into a small pool, with the second tier falling several more feet into the creek. Just ahead is High Bridge, a wide metal bridge spanning 120 feet above a slot canyon. There are plenty of areas to sit and enjoy the scenery before heading back. Return the same way.

For a longer hike, continue for another 2.7 miles past High Bridge to Tunnel Falls (175 ft.).

DIRECTIONS TO TRAILHEAD

From Portland, take I-84 East for 38 miles to the Eagle Creek Recreation Area Exit 41.

Turn right and drive 0.5 miles to the trailhead.

DRIVE TIME FROM PORTLAND
45 minutes

Photos, left to right from top: Eagle Creek; Metlako Falls; Punch Bowl Falls; section of trail with cables.

EAGLE CREEK TO HIGH BRIDGE

Photos, left to right from top: Eagle Creek; narrow gorge above the creek; High Bridge; Eagle Creek; mossy forest.

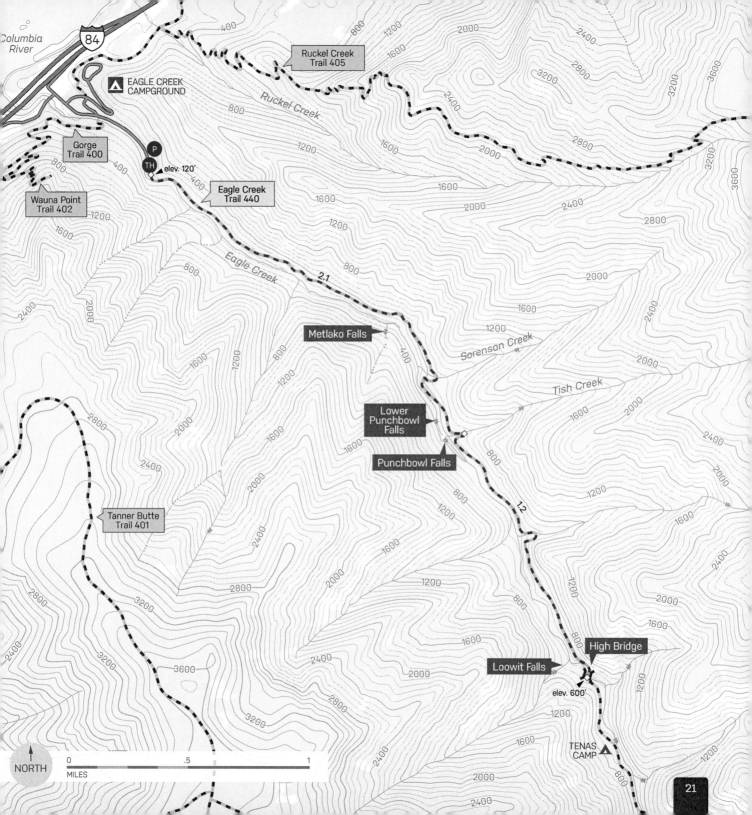

Columbia River

84

Ruckel Creek Trail 405

EAGLE CREEK CAMPGROUND

Ruckel Creek

P
TH
elev. 120'

Gorge Trail 400

Eagle Creek Trail 440

Wauna Point Trail 402

Eagle Creek

2.1

Metlako Falls

Sorenson Creek

Lower Punchbowl Falls

Tish Creek

Punchbowl Falls

Tanner Butte Trail 401

1.2

High Bridge

Loowit Falls

elev. 600'

TENAS CAMP

NORTH

0   .5   1
MILES

Herman Creek

A lesser-known alternative to the popular Eagle Creek trail, the Herman Creek trail doesn't have as many waterfalls, but it also doesn't have the steep trail drop-offs or the crowds.

All of these hikes begin at the same trailhead, located at the west end of Herman Creek campground. The trail begins in a mixed forest of Douglas fir and bigleaf maple trees covered heavily with lichens and moss. After crossing uphill to an open power line section, stay to the right on the path and continue on the trail through a bit more forest before encountering a stretch of moss covered boulders, some with cave-like openings at their base which look like they could be home to elves, trolls, or other forest folk. Continue a short distance to a signed trail junction.

Herman Creek Trail: At the signed trail junction, stay to the left to continue on the Herman Creek Trail. The trail parallels Herman Creek, but the creek is only occasionally visible from the trail, which is high above on the canyon wall.

Following an old gravel roadbed, continue straight, passing trail junctions for the Gordon Creek and Nick Eaton Trails. A tall wispy waterfall, Nick Eaton Falls, is named after nearby Nick Eaton Ridge. Past the waterfall, the trail goes through an open section with old and twisted Oregon white oak trees. A wilderness entry sign (no permits needed) is just before lovely Camp Creek. Continue for about another mile to the junction with the Casey Creek trail. A large primitive campsite is a great place to stop before heading back. Return the same way.

Pinnacles & Dry Creek Falls: At the signed trail junction, fork to the right on the Herman Creek Bridge Trail. Heading downhill towards Herman Creek, which can be heard below, the trail crosses a long metal footbridge, which offers great views of Herman Creek in both directions. This is the only time you'll be near the creek, so it's worth spending a few minutes taking in the views from the bridge or exploring the banks of the creek below.

About one mile from the creek, turn right on the Pacific Crest Trail (PCT), a 2,650-mile trail that runs from Mexico to Canada through California, Oregon, and Washington. Continue through alternating forested and rocky talus slopes, with occasional openings to views of the Columbia River and the Washington side of the Gorge, to Pacific Crest Falls, which cascades down the hillside above and below the trail.

In early spring, the water flow is at its peak, making the waterfall a nice feature of this hike. Continue on the trail for about 250 yards to the pinnacles. A small rocky path leads to a nice open area at the base of the spires. Spend a bit of time exploring around the spires – there are several small paths leading up and around the bases of these fascinating structures. Turn around here, or continue for another 1.3 miles to Dry Creek Falls, a relatively unknown waterfall that is anything but dry. Return the same way.

HERMAN CREEK TO CASEY CREEK

DISTANCE: 8.6 miles (roundtrip)
ELEVATION GAIN: 1,600 ft.
DIFFICULTY: moderate

HERMAN CREEK PINNACLES

DISTANCE: 4.8 miles (roundtrip)
ELEVATION GAIN: 1,020 ft.
DIFFICULTY: moderate

DRY CREEK FALLS

DISTANCE: 7.4 miles (roundtrip)
ELEVATION GAIN: 1,200 ft.
DIFFICULTY: moderate

HIKE TYPES: out and back

TRAIL: packed dirt, rock

OPEN: all year

BEST TIME OF YEAR: April - June and Oct. - Nov.

FEATURES: forest, creek, waterfall, geologic features

FEES/PERMITS: Northwest Forest Pass required

AGENCY: Columbia River Gorge National Scenic Area

DIRECTIONS TO TRAILHEAD

From Portland, take I-84 East for 40 miles to Cascade Locks Exit 44.

Continue east on Wa Na Pa Street through Cascade Locks for 1.5 miles.

Turn right on Frontage Road, and continue for 1.7 miles (going over the highway and making a sharp left turn) to a sign for the Herman Creek Campground.

Turn right, going uphill into the campground, and stay to the right for the day use area parking lot.

If the road to the campground is gated, park next to the Frontage Road and walk up the campground road.

DRIVE TIME FROM PORTLAND
50 minutes

Photos, left to right from top: moss-covered boulders; Herman Creek; Nick Eaton Falls; pinnacles.

HERMAN CR. TR. NO. 406
GORTON CR. TR. NO. 408 0.7
GORGE TR. NO. 400   0.7
NICK EATON TR. NO. 447 0.8

HERMAN CREEK

Photos, left to right from top: Herman Creek; old-growth tree with moss; trail junction sign; sunlight filtering through the forest; bridge over Herman Creek.

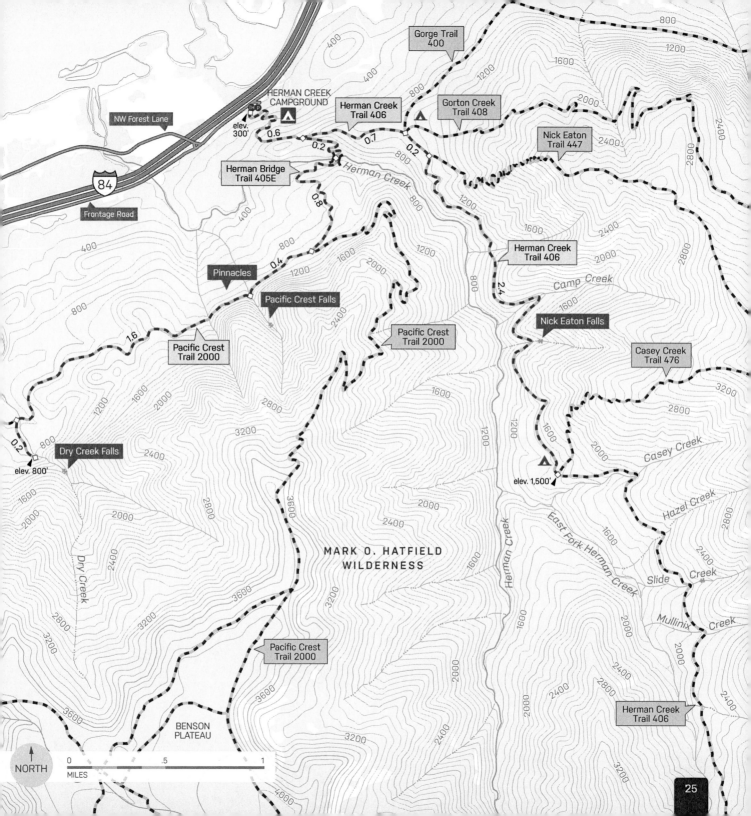

Gorge Trail 400

NW Forest Lane

HERMAN CREEK CAMPGROUND

elev. 300'

Herman Creek Trail 406

Gorton Creek Trail 408

0.6

0.2

0.7

0.2

Nick Eaton Trail 447

Herman Bridge Trail 405E

Herman Creek

0.8

Herman Creek Trail 406

Frontage Road

Pinnacles

0.4

Pacific Crest Falls

Camp Creek

2.4

Nick Eaton Falls

Pacific Crest Trail 2000

Pacific Crest Trail 2000

Casey Creek Trail 476

1.6

0.2

Dry Creek Falls

elev. 800'

elev. 1,500'

Casey Creek

Hazel Creek

MARK O. HATFIELD WILDERNESS

Herman Creek

East Fork Herman Creek

Slide Creek

Mullinix Creek

Pacific Crest Trail 2000

Herman Creek Trail 406

BENSON PLATEAU

NORTH

0   .5   1
MILES

25

McCall Point + Rowena Plateau

Located east of the Cascades on the drier side of the Columbia River Gorge, Tom McCall Point and Rowena Plateau are a top destination for wildflower displays each April and May.

Each spring, the the meadows and hillsides surrounding Tom McCall Point are transformed by wildflowers, creating a view dominated by yellow balsamroot and blue lupines with accents of red paintbrush, blue bachelor buttons, and white yarrow. And, of course, wide open vistas of the Columbia River and Gorge are constantly visible.

This landscape was carved by ancient lava flows and floods and contains significant evidence of the Ice Age floods, with "kolk" lakes, hummock-like mounds, and eight layers of basalt in the cliffs lining the river.

Both of these hikes are on lands owned by the Nature Conservancy, which helps protect this place of special ecological significance. Note that dogs are not allowed on the trails in this area, and visitors should beware of ticks, rattlesnakes, and poison oak. Starting in the spring, Nature Conservancy volunteers lead interpretive hikes.

Rowena Plateau hike: From the parking area, cross the roadway to the trailhead for Rowena Plateau. The trail leads gently downhill for this hike, returning the same way. After a short distance, a side trail heads to a great viewpoint of the Columbia River. On the main trail, 1/2 mile in is Rowena Pond.

Side trails lead to the pond, but watch out for poison oak, which is abundant in this area. Continue on the main trail to the end, with a viewpoint looking west towards the town of Mosier. Return the same way.

McCall Point hike: This trail is only open from May 1st to October 31st. Begin at the Rowena Crest trailhead and continue for about 2/10 of a mile to an intersection with an old road, which leads to a viewpoint of the Columbia River. Back on the main trail, at 1/2 mile in you will reach the sign for the Tom McCall Point Trail. The path now climbs and reaches slopes overlooking Rowena Plateau. Views across the river include the town of Lyle, Washington, with Mount Adams beyond it. And to the west you'll see Mount Defiance and the Columbia River heading through a narrower section of the Gorge.

The trail gets steeper as it switchbacks up the hillside through alternating sections of scrub oaks and open grassy areas. At the top, the hill flattens out into a small meadow area with panoramic views. Return the same way.

MCCALL POINT TRAIL

DISTANCE: 3.4 miles (roundtrip)

ELEVATION GAIN: 1,070 ft.

DIFFICULTY: moderate

HIKE TYPE: out and back

OPEN: May 1 - October 31

BEST TIME OF YEAR: May

FEATURES: wildflowers

FEES/PERMITS: none

AGENCY: The Nature Conservancy

Note: Dogs are not allowed on the trails in this area

ROWENA PLATEAU TRAIL

DISTANCE: 2.2 miles (roundtrip)

ELEVATION GAIN: 300 ft.

DIFFICULTY: easy

HIKE TYPE: out and back

OPEN: year round

BEST TIME OF YEAR: April - May

DIRECTIONS TO TRAILHEAD

From Portland, drive east on I-84 for 67 miles to US-30 Mosier Exit 69.

Turn right and follow the Historic Columbia River Highway US-30 for 6.7 miles.

Turn right at the sign for Rowena Crest.

DRIVE TIME FROM PORTLAND
1 hour 30 minutes

Photos, left to right from top: Balsamroot flowers and the Columbia River; Tom McCall Point; near the top of the point, view of the Columbia River from Rowena Plateau.

MCCALL POINT + ROWENA PLATEAU

Photos, left to right from top: Rowena Plateau and the Columbia River; Old Columbia River Highway; wildflowers in early May; oak trees, path on the way up to Tom McCall Point.

LYLE,
WASHINGTON

Columbia River

200

400

400

400

200

30

HISTORIC COLUMBIA RIVER HWY

600

600

ROWENA
PLATEAU

elev. 450'

1.1

400

400

600

600

Rowena
Plateau Trail

600

200

P

TH
elev. 700'

Rowena Crest
Viewpoint

800

800

600

400

400

McCall
Point Trail

800

800

30

400

1.7

600

1000

1000

1200

600

800

1200

1400

McCALL
POINT

elev. 1,722'

1400

1600

NORTH

0   .5   1

MILES

Crater
Lake

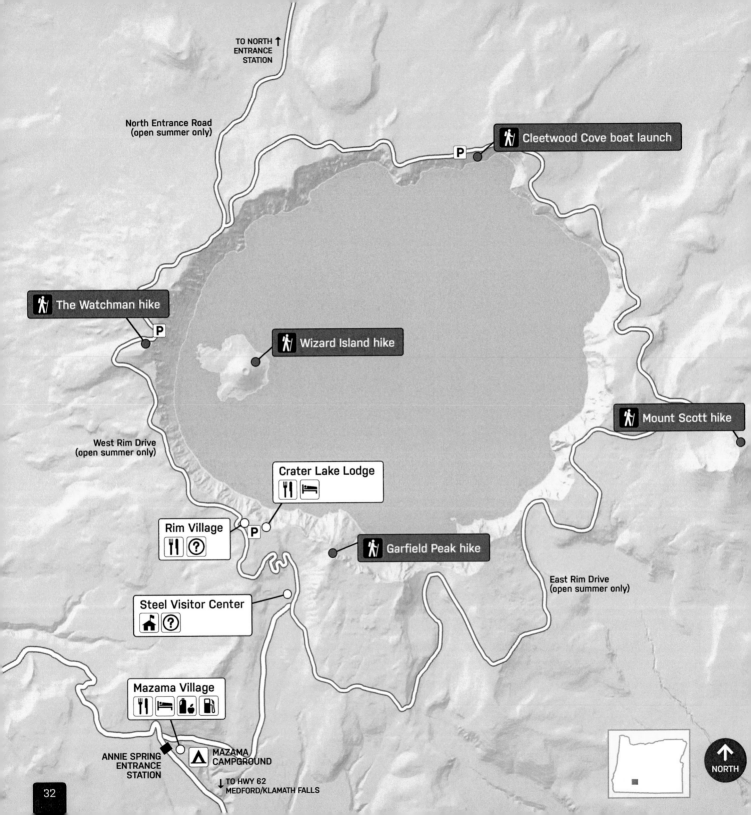

TO NORTH ↑
ENTRANCE
STATION

North Entrance Road
(open summer only)

P 🚶 Cleetwood Cove boat launch

🚶 The Watchman hike
P

🚶 Wizard Island hike

🚶 Mount Scott hike

West Rim Drive
(open summer only)

Crater Lake Lodge
🍴 🛏

Rim Village
🍴 ❓
P

🚶 Garfield Peak hike

East Rim Drive
(open summer only)

Steel Visitor Center
🏠 ❓

Mazama Village
🍴 🛏 🍎 ⛽

ANNIE SPRING
ENTRANCE
STATION

△ MAZAMA
CAMPGROUND

↓ TO HWY 62
MEDFORD/KLAMATH FALLS

NORTH

Crater Lake was formed when Mount Mazama (12,000 ft.) exploded about 7,700 years ago, leaving a caldera that eventually filled with rainwater and snowmelt to form the lake.

Established in 1902, Crater Lake National Park protects what is considered the cleanest large body of water in the world. Known for its brilliant blue color, the lake is 4-1/2 to 6 miles wide, and is the deepest in the U.S. with a depth of 1,943 feet.

The lake is surrounded by 90 miles of trails for hiking, ranging from easy walks along the rim, to ascents up rocky peaks with panoramic views. For a truly unique experience, take the boat ride to Wizard Island, the iconic cinder cone located in the lake, and hike up to the top of a volcano inside a volcano. Trails are usually snow-free by mid-June, but higher elevations may see snow until mid-July.

Winter is a long season at Crater Lake, with an average annual snowfall of 44 feet, usually beginning in October. Park rangers lead interpretive snowshoe hikes, or you can snowshoe on your own. Winter is also the only time of year that camping within a view of the lake is allowed. To experience this unique winter camping opportunity, pick up a free backcountry permit at the park's headquarters, grab your backpack, and hike in on snowshoes or skis. Make sure to check the weather forecast first though, since the lake is only visible about 50% of the time in the winter.

Steel Visitor Center; Phantom Ship as seen from the boat ride; The Castle.

Watchman Peak + Wizard Island

The trail to the top of Wizard Island offers the unique experience of hiking on a volcano inside a volcano, while ranger-led treks at sunset to the top of Watchman Peak offer panoramic views from the decks of a fire lookout.

Wizard Island was formed about 7,300 years ago, emerging from Crater Lake in a shower of fiery cinders that piled into a symmetrical cone, with lava flowing around the island and forming its shores.

The only way to get to Wizard Island is via a ranger-narrated boat tour, departing multiple times each day (weather permitting) from Cleetwood Cove. Purchase a ticket in advance online, or during a visit from automated kiosks inside Crater Lake Lodge and the Annie Creek Gift Shop. Arrive at least 45 minutes before the boat departure time for the 1.1 mile hike down to the boat dock.

Cleetwood Cove: Located on the north side of Crater Lake, Cleetwood Cove is the only lake-level access, with a large boat dock for the park's tours. Swimming in the chilly waters at the cove is allowed from the shoreline near the end of the trail.

Take the 1.1 mile trail down to the boat dock via several long – and steep – switchbacks, losing about 700 feet of elevation on the way. The trail is wide, with loose rock, and offers views of Mount Scott to the east. Save plenty of energy for the return hike up this steep trail.

Wizard Island: Arrive at the boat dock at Governors Bay and take the Summit trail to the right. The trail crosses through an area thick with lava rock before winding its way around the slopes of the island and up to the summit. At the top, the trail continues all the way around the rim, with ancient whitebark pines along the sides of the crater. Side trails from the top lead into the center of the caldera, known as the Witches Cauldron. Be on time for the return boat ride, or face a hefty fine from the national park. Depending on the type of ticket purchased, the boat ride may include a full ranger-narrated tour of the lake, including circling around Phantom Ship, a small island made of 400,000-year-old lava, and possibly a sighting of The Old Man of the Lake, a hemlock log that has been floating vertically on Crater Lake for over 100 years.

Watchman Peak: A prominent point on the west side of Crater Lake's rim, Watchman Peak offers spectacular views from the decks of a fire lookout, including Wizard Island directly below, and of the Cascades to the west. Built in 1932, the fire lookout is still used by rangers. Sunset tours led by park rangers are usually available in the summer. Park at the Watchman Overlook viewpoint (on the north side of Watchman Peak), 4 miles north of Rim Village.

WIZARD ISLAND
Photos, left to right from top: ancient whitebark pine trees on the summit rim; lava rock on Wizard Island, view of Crater Lake from the trail; Wizard Island's caldera.

WIZARD ISLAND
DISTANCE: 2.2 miles (roundtrip)
ELEVATION GAIN: 760 ft.
DIFFICULTY: moderate
HIKE TYPE: out and back
FEATURES: geological features; panoramic views

CLEETWOOD COVE
DISTANCE: 2.2 miles (roundtrip)
ELEVATION GAIN: 700 ft.
DIFFICULTY: moderate
HIKE TYPE: out and back

WATCHMAN PEAK
DISTANCE: 1.6 miles (roundtrip)
ELEVATION GAIN: 420 ft.
DIFFICULTY: easy
HIKE TYPE: out and back
FEATURES: panoramic views, fire lookout

OPEN: mid-July - Sept.
BEST TIME OF YEAR: mid-July - Sept.
FEES/PERMITS: National Park entrance fee
AGENCY: Crater Lake National Park
NOTE: Dogs are not allowed on the trails at Crater Lake National Park

DIRECTIONS TO CRATER LAKE

From Portland, take I-5 South for 113 miles to Highway 58 Oakridge / Klamath Falls Exit 188.

Continue on Highway 58 for 86 miles to Highway 97 South.

Continue on Highway 97 for 18 miles to Highway 138.

Turn right on Highway 138 and continue for 30 miles.

Turn left at the entrance to Crater Lake National Park and continue for 15 miles to Rim Village.

DRIVE TIME FROM PORTLAND
5 hours

WATCHMAN PEAK
Photos, left to right from top: view from the top of Watchman Peak; former fire lookout at the summit; the trail is wide, with a gentle grade; views of Crater Lake on the way up; sunset view to the west.

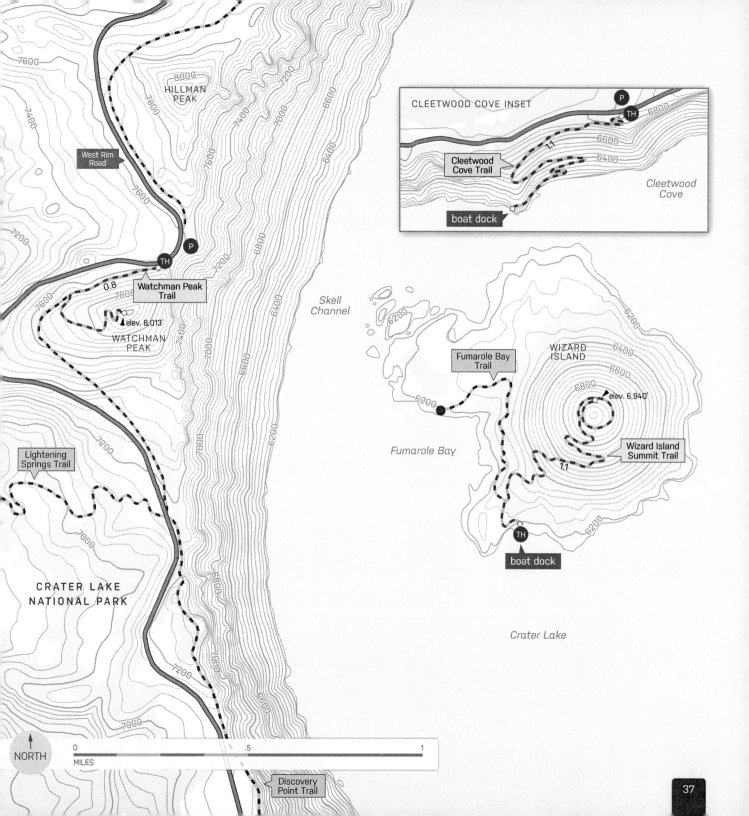

CLEETWOOD COVE INSET

Cleetwood Cove Trail

Cleetwood Cove

boat dock

HILLMAN PEAK

West Rim Road

Watchman Peak Trail

0.8

▲ elev. 8,013'

WATCHMAN PEAK

Skell Channel

WIZARD ISLAND

Fumarole Bay Trail

▲ elev. 6,940'

Wizard Island Summit Trail

1.1

Lightening Springs Trail

Fumarole Bay

boat dock

CRATER LAKE NATIONAL PARK

Crater Lake

NORTH

0   .5   1
MILES

Discovery Point Trail

Garfield Peak + Mount Scott

Two of the park's highest points, Mount Scott and Garfield Peak offer outstanding panoramic views of Crater Lake, the Klamath Basin, and the Cascades.

Garfield Peak: Located directly east of Crater Lake Lodge along the caldera rim, Garfield Peak towers above Rim Village. Named in honor of James R. Garfield, former U.S. Secretary of the Interior, during his visit to the park in 1907. Usually covered in snow from October to July, check with the park's ranger station for current conditions. As with other trails at Crater Lake National Park, dogs are not allowed on this trail.

To reach the trailhead, follow the paved path past the lodge. The rocky trail climbs along the side of Garfield Peak, with hemlocks and Shasta red fir trees along the lower portions of the trail. Along the way up, openings in the trees provide views of the Klamath Basin to the south. Pikas (small mammals with rounded ears that are related to rabbits) and yellow-bellied marmots live in the rocky slopes along the trail. Heading back towards the lake, the trail follows the steep walls of the rim before turning and beginning the final ascent near the 8,054' summit. Whitebark pines and subalpine fir trees dominate the upper portions of the peak. Panoramic views include Crater Lake and Phantom Ship (a small island in the southeast part of the lake), Mount Thielsen with its pointy spire to the north, and Mount Scott to the east. In July, alpine wildflowers bloom along the upper portions of the trail. Return the same way.

Mount Scott: Located on the east side of Crater Lake, Mount Scott is the highest point in the park (8,929 ft.), with a working fire lookout at the summit. Usually covered in snow from October to July, check with the park's ranger station for current conditions. As with other trails at Crater Lake National Park, dogs are not allowed on this trail.

To reach the trailhead, take the East Rim Road for 14 miles from the Steel Visitor Center to a roadside pullout for parking. The first section of trail is relatively flat and located beside an open pumice field with views of Mount Scott and its summit ridge. After about a quarter mile, the trail begins a gradual ascent along the southwestern side of Mount Scott through a forest of mountain hemlock, with whitebark pines and Shasta red firs. Climbing more steeply, the trail switchbacks up with views of Crater Lake to the west and the Klamath Basin to the south. Winding around to the summit ridge, the trail follows the ridge to the north to the fire lookout. From the ridge, a full panoramic view of Crater Lake fills the horizon. In mid- to late July, alpine wildflowers bloom along the slopes. Return the same way.

GARFIELD PEAK
DISTANCE: 3.4 miles (roundtrip)
ELEVATION GAIN: 1,010 ft.
DIFFICULTY: moderate
HIKE TYPE: out and back

MOUNT SCOTT
DISTANCE: 5 miles (roundtrip)
ELEVATION GAIN: 1,250 ft.
DIFFICULTY: moderate
HIKE TYPE: out and back

OPEN: mid-July - Sept.
BEST TIME OF YEAR: mid-July - Sept.
FEATURES: geological formations; panoramic views
FEES/PERMITS: National Park entrance fee
AGENCY: Crater Lake National Park
NOTE: Dogs are not allowed on the trails at Crater Lake National Park

DIRECTIONS TO CRATER LAKE

From Portland, take I-5 South for 113 miles to Highway 58 Oakridge / Klamath Falls Exit 188.

Continue on Highway 58 for 86 miles to Highway 97 South.

Continue on Highway 97 for 18 miles to Highway 138.

Turn right on Highway 138 and continue for 30 miles.

Turn left at the entrance to Crater Lake National Park and continue for 15 miles to Rim Village.

DRIVE TIME FROM PORTLAND
5 hours

MOUNT SCOTT
Photos, left to right from top: panoramic view of Crater Lake; fire lookout in use; view to the south of the Klamath Basin; Mount Scott's saddle; section of trail.

GARFIELD PEAK
Photos, left to right from top: view of Crater Lake and Wizard Island; view to the southwest; typical section of rocky trail; view of Crater Lake with Mount Scott in the distance and Phantom Ship in the lake.

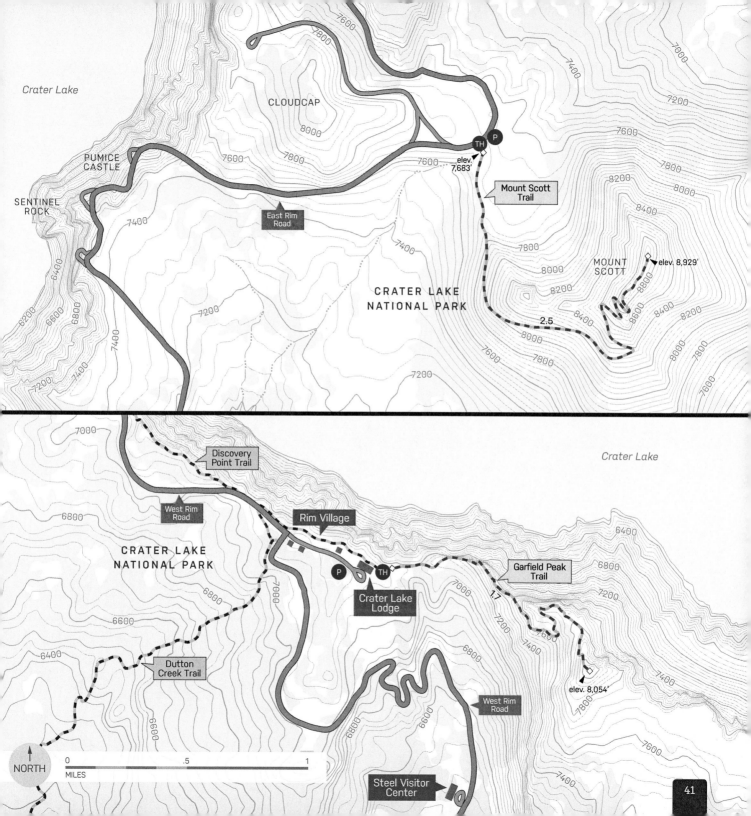

Crater Lake

CLOUDCAP

8000

7600

7800

7400

PUMICE
CASTLE

SENTINEL
ROCK

7400

6400

East Rim
Road

7400

7200

elev.
7,683'

TH   P

Mount Scott
Trail

7800

8000

8200

8400

MOUNT
SCOTT

elev. 8,929'

CRATER LAKE
NATIONAL PARK

2.5

7200

Discovery
Point Trail

West Rim
Road

Crater Lake

CRATER LAKE
NATIONAL PARK

6800

6600

Rim Village

P   TH

Crater Lake
Lodge

Garfield Peak
Trail

1.7

elev. 8,054'

Dutton
Creek Trail

6400

West Rim
Road

Steel Visitor
Center

NORTH

0   .5   1
MILES

Mount
Hood

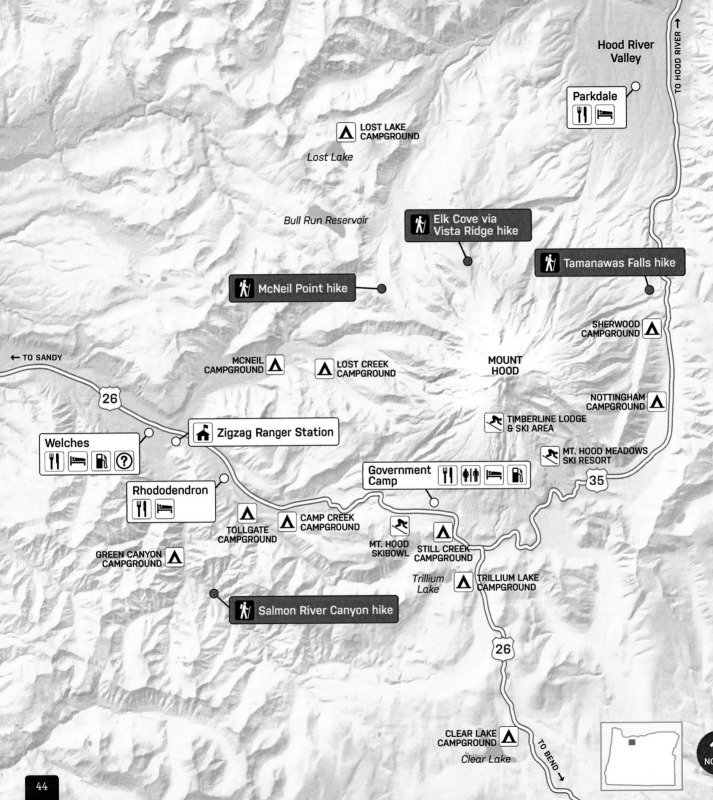

Hood River Valley

TO HOOD RIVER

Parkdale

LOST LAKE CAMPGROUND

Lost Lake

Bull Run Reservoir

Elk Cove via Vista Ridge hike

Tamanawas Falls hike

McNeil Point hike

SHERWOOD CAMPGROUND

MOUNT HOOD

← TO SANDY

26

MCNEIL CAMPGROUND

LOST CREEK CAMPGROUND

NOTTINGHAM CAMPGROUND

Welches

TIMBERLINE LODGE & SKI AREA

Zigzag Ranger Station

MT. HOOD MEADOWS SKI RESORT

Rhododendron

Government Camp

35

TOLLGATE CAMPGROUND

CAMP CREEK CAMPGROUND

MT. HOOD SKIBOWL

STILL CREEK CAMPGROUND

GREEN CANYON CAMPGROUND

Trillium Lake

TRILLIUM LAKE CAMPGROUND

Salmon River Canyon hike

26

TO BEND →

CLEAR LAKE CAMPGROUND

Clear Lake

NORTH

Named Wy'east by the Native American Multnomah tribe, Mount Hood is located in the Cascade Mountain Range, about 50 miles east of Portland. At 11,240 ft., Mount Hood is Oregon's highest mountain and has eleven active glaciers.

A dormant volcano, Mount Hood's last major eruption was around 300 years ago, yet it still vents sulfur near the summit and is considered a likely candidate to become active again.

With nearly 1,000 miles of trails in the region, hikes range from lower elevation rambles in temperate rain forest with waterfalls and streams, to higher altitude trails with alpine meadows and rocky ridges. Alpine areas are usually accessible from late-July until the autumn snows begin in October or November. Lower-lying areas can be accessible year-round, depending on snow levels.

The Timberline Trail circumnavigates Mount Hood on approximately 40 miles of trail. Eleven of those miles are shared with the Pacific Crest Trail. Timberline refers to the tree line on the mountain, which is generally at about 6,000 ft. elevation. Timberline Lodge, located on the south side of the mountain at the base of the Palmer Glacier, is a National Historic Landmark built in the 1930s.

Averaging 400 inches of snow each year, Mount Hood has six ski areas, including year-round skiing at Timberline. Snowshoeing is a popular alternative to hiking when the trails are covered with snow.

Footbridges on the Salmon River Canyon and Tamanawas Falls trails.

Hike along the Bald Mountain ridge on Mount Hood's northwest side, passing through wildflower-filled alpine meadows to the McNeil Point stone shelter just below the Sandy and Glisan glaciers.

DISTANCE: 9.6 miles (roundtrip)

ELEVATION GAIN: 2,220 ft.

DIFFICULTY: difficult

HIKE TYPE: out and back

TRAIL: packed dirt and rock

OPEN: mid-July - mid-Oct.

BEST TIME OF YEAR: Aug. - Oct.

FEATURES: forest, alpine meadows, mountain views, glaciers

FEES/PERMITS: Northwest Forest Pass required

AGENCY: Hood River Ranger District, Mount Hood National Forest

Starting at the Top Spur trailhead, the first several miles are in a Douglas fir and mountain hemlock cathedral forest, with an understory of huckleberries that ripen in August. Less than a quarter-mile from the trailhead, turn right at the junction with the Pacific Crest Trail, and at a three-trail junction a short distance later, bear left (somewhat uphill) on the Timberline Trail. An optional (center) trail loops around Bald Mountain, providing big views of Mount Hood and adding just under a half-mile to the hike. A short distance ahead, fill out a Mount Hood Wilderness permit at the self-registration station.

Continue on the Timberline Trail to the wildflower-filled slopes of Bald Mountain Ridge. Openings in the forest provide stunning views of Mount Hood, with towering Yocum Ridge to the right, and the valley of the Muddy Fork of the Sandy River far below. Wildflowers in the alpine meadows include red paintbrush, blue lupine, avalanche lilies, western pasqueflower, beargrass, heather, and pink spiraea.

At a scenic alpine area with tarns (ponds created by snow melt), stay right at all junctions, hiking through forest, past rock slides and up a ridge beside Ladd Creek.

At times, the trail is hard to distinguish as it goes through thick shrubbery. Just past timberline, snowfields can linger on the rocky slopes all year. Cross the snowfields and continue to the McNeil Point stone shelter, built in the 1930s by the Civilian Conservation Corps.

Take in amazing views in all directions, including Mount Rainier, Mount St. Helens and Mount Adams. For a closer look at the Sandy and Glisan glaciers, continue on the trail above the shelter for a few hundred feet. After soaking in this glorious high mountain region, return the same way.

Conditions on this high exposed area can change quickly, so be prepared with warm layers of clothing and rain gear. A good general rule is that if the mountain is completely socked in, it's best to do this hike another day. It's easy to get lost in high mountain terrain, and the effort to get there is better rewarded when there are views all around.

DIRECTIONS TO TRAILHEAD

From Portland: drive 42 miles east on U.S. 26 to Zigzag.

Across from the Zigzag Ranger District, turn left onto East Lolo Pass Road.

Continue for 4.2 miles, then fork right on paved road 1825.

After 0.7 miles, just before a bridge over the Sandy River, go straight on Road 1828 (paved single lane road with turnouts).

Continue 5.6 miles and fork to the right on gravel Road 118, for 1.5 miles to the Top Spur Trailhead.

DRIVE TIME FROM PORTLAND
1 hour 40 minutes

Photos, left to right from top: panoramic views from above McNeil Point Shelter; tarn below McNeil Point; up-close view of Mount Hood; trail just below treeline.

MCNEIL POINT

Photos, left to right from top: Bald Mountain Ridge; alpine wildflowers; McNeil Point stone shelter; fall color on Bald Mountain Ridge; tarns below McNeil Point.

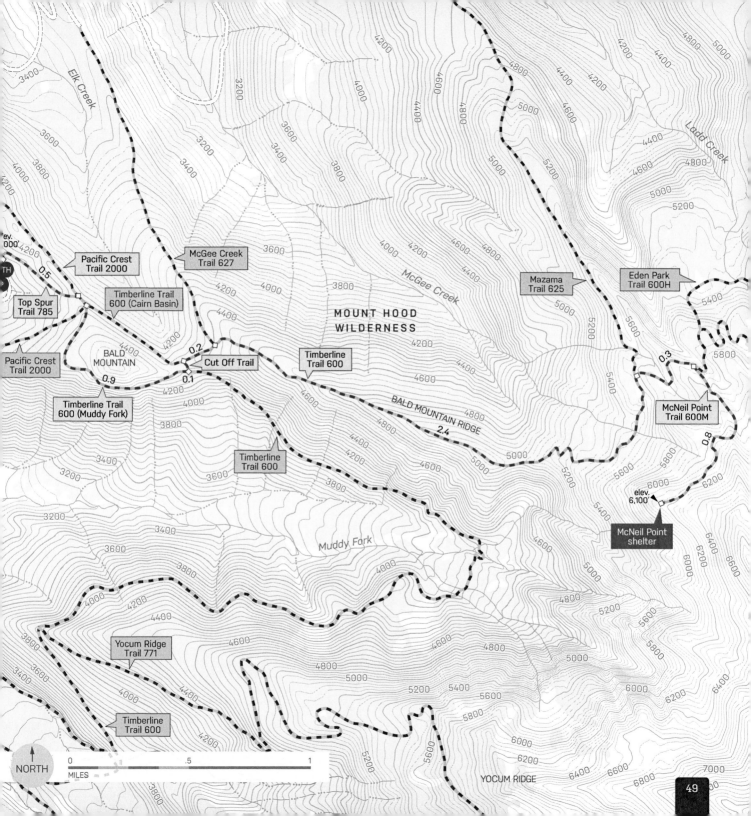

MOUNT HOOD
WILDERNESS

Elk Creek

Ladd Creek

McGee Creek

BALD MOUNTAIN RIDGE

Muddy Fork

YOCUM RIDGE

elev.
6,000'

ev.
000'

TH

0.5

0.2

0.1

0.9

0.3

0.8

2.4

elev.
6,100'

Pacific Crest Trail 2000

McGee Creek Trail 627

Timberline Trail 600 (Cairn Basin)

Top Spur Trail 785

Pacific Crest Trail 2000

Cut Off Trail

Timberline Trail 600

Mazama Trail 625

Eden Park Trail 600H

McNeil Point Trail 600M

Timberline Trail 600 (Muddy Fork)

Timberline Trail 600

McNeil Point shelter

Yocum Ridge Trail 771

Timberline Trail 600

BALD
MOUNTAIN

NORTH

0   .5   1
MILES

49

Elk Cove via Vista Ridge

Located on the north side of Mount Hood, Elk Cove is a quiet place with cascading streams, wildflower meadows, and occasional views of Mount Hood's rugged upper face.

The north side of Mount Hood is visited less than other parts of the mountain, largely due to the longer drives required to reach trailheads. Several ridge trails exist in this area, with the Vista Ridge trail providing the least steep entry to Mount Hood's subalpine areas. Access to the Vista Ridge trail is a long drive on decent mountain roads, with great views of Mount Hood along the way.

The trail begins in a mixed forest for 0.2 miles to a junction with the old Vista Ridge trail. From here, the green forest soon ends, and for the next 2 miles, the hike is though an eerie section of burned forest from the 2012 Dollar Lake wildfire. Fireweed and avalanche lilies bloom on the open forest floor. The trail climbs gently, with several switchbacks leading to the top of the ridge.

After approximately 2.5 miles, reach a junction with the Timberline Trail. Turn left and continue past a trail junction at 0.3 miles for Eden Park, then in another 0.3 miles, a trail junction for Cairn Basin, and another 0.3 miles at a trail junction for Pinnacle Ridge.

Now in a more open forest, the ridge provides panoramic views of distant Cascades, including Mount Adams, Mount Saint Helens, and Mount Rainier.

Cross several small creeks, and past meadows that are filled with Paintbrush, lupines, asters, and heathers in late summer. Also at this time of year, Western Pasque Flower's seed heads sway in the wind. This peculiar wildflower is also known by several other names, including "Old Man on the Mountain" and "Hippy on a Stick".

The trail goes through several smaller sections of burned forest, and around a few large rock slide sections.

A side trail to Dollar Lake is hard to locate, but is usually marked with a small rock cairn. This side trail goes steeply uphill next to a lovely drainage area filled with wildflowers, to tiny Dollar Lake. Adventurous hikers can continue from here to Barrett Spur.

Back on the main trail, continue towards Eden Park. Wildflower meadows fill the open spaces, and the rugged north side of Mount Hood makes occasional appearances.

DISTANCE: 8 miles (roundtrip)

ELEVATION GAIN: 2,000 ft.

DIFFICULTY: moderate to difficult

HIKE TYPE: out and back

TRAIL: packed dirt and rock

OPEN: July - Nov.

BEST TIME OF YEAR: late July - early Sept.

FEATURES: wildflower meadows, mountain views

FEES/PERMITS: Northwest Forest Pass required

AGENCY: Hood River Ranger District, Mount Hood National Forest

DIRECTIONS TO TRAILHEAD

From Portland: drive 42 miles east on U.S. 26 to Zigzag.

Across from the Zigzag Ranger District, turn left onto East Lolo Pass Road.

Continue on Lolo Pass Road for 10.7 miles, and take the second right onto FS 18 (signed for Lost Lake).

Continue for 10.5 miles (the first 5.5 are gravel).

Turn right at a hairpin curve onto FS 16. (signed for the Vista Ridge Trail).

Continue for 5.4 miles and turn right at a large intersection onto FS 1650.

The trailhead is 3.6 miles ahead, at the end of the road.

DRIVE TIME FROM PORTLAND
2 hours 15 minutes

Photos, left to right from top: the rugged north face of Mount Hood, wildflower-filled ravine next to the Dollar Lake side trail; Coe Creek, burned section of forest.

ELK COVE VIA VISTA RIDGE

Photos, left to right from top: views of Mount St. Helens and Mount Adams from the ridge; wildflower meadows at Elk Cove; western pasqueflower; creek at Elk Cove; stream in a ravine.

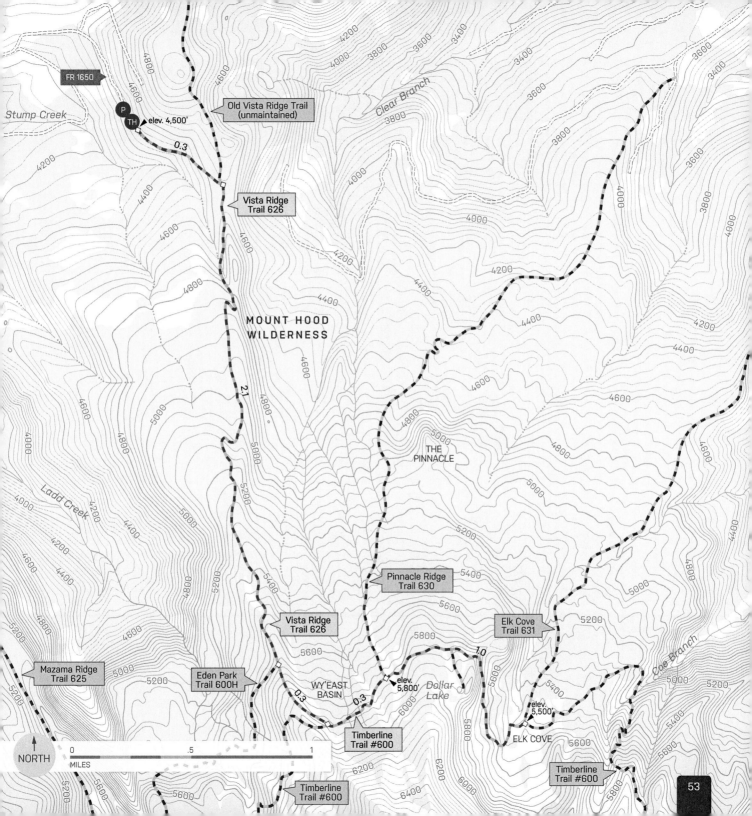

FR 1650

Stump Creek

P
TH ▶ elev. 4,500'

0.3

◀ Old Vista Ridge Trail
(unmaintained)

Clear Branch

Vista Ridge
Trail 626

MOUNT HOOD
WILDERNESS

2.1

Ladd Creek

THE
PINNACLE

Pinnacle Ridge
Trail 630 ▶

Vista Ridge
Trail 626

Elk Cove
Trail 631 ▶

Mazama Ridge
Trail 625

Eden Park
Trail 600H

WY'EAST
BASIN

1.0

Dollar
Lake

0.3

elev.
5,800'

0.3

elev.
5,500'

Coe Branch

ELK COVE

Timberline
Trail #600

Timberline
Trail #600

NORTH

0   .5   1

MILES

Timberline
Trail #600

Tamanawas Falls

The beauty of the mossy green Cold Spring Creek canyon and 100 ft. tall Tamanawas Falls makes this one of the most picturesque hikes on the east side of Mount Hood.

DISTANCE: 4.2 miles (roundtrip)

ELEVATION GAIN: 900 ft.

DIFFICULTY: easy to moderate

HIKE TYPE: loop

TRAIL: packed dirt and rock

OPEN: May - Nov., depending on snow levels

BEST TIME OF YEAR: June - Oct.

FEATURES: waterfall, creek, forest

FEES/PERMITS: Northwest Forest Pass required

AGENCY: Hood River Ranger District, Mount Hood National Forest

A Native American word, Tamanawas means "friendly spirit guide." It's not hard to imagine friendly spirits enjoying the breathtaking scenery here.

Most people begin at the East Fork trailhead for a shorter hike, but for a longer, much less crowded hike, begin at the Elk Meadows trailhead to the north, parking at the Polallie picnic area. The trailhead is not well marked, but is easy to find. Look directly across the highway from the parking lot for a trail heading uphill.

For the first 1.5 miles, travel through heavy forest with a mix of western red cedar and Douglas fir. Occasionally, the forest opens enough to catch a peek of Mount Adams to the north. After 1.3 miles is a trail junction with the Tamanawas Falls Tie Trail (#650B). Turn here and descend for just over .25 miles to a junction with the Tamanawas Trail (#650A). Turn right and pass through an area filled with extra large boulders, following the trail to Tamanawas Falls (100 ft.). Traversing across a steep talus slope, it is possible to reach a small amphitheater behind the falls.

From the falls, return to the junction and stay on the Tamanawas Falls Trail as it meanders along Cold Spring Creek, a tributary of the East Fork Hood River. This section of the hike is the prettiest, with plenty of spots to access the mossy banks of the creek. For the return loop to the Elk Meadows trailhead, turn left at a junction just uphill from a rustic bridge crossing the creek. This section of trail traverses up and down the hillside several times parallel to the highway, although it is far enough above it to feel somewhat secluded. There are a couple of small creek crossings, and waterproof boots will be handy during higher water levels.

For a shorter hike, park at the East Fork trailhead located about a mile south of the Polallie picnic area. From here, it's just over half a mile to the Tamanawas Trail, and includes a newer footbridge over the raging waters of the East Fork Hood River.

DIRECTIONS TO TRAILHEAD

From Portland, take I-84 East for 62 miles to Hood River.

Take Exit 64 for Highway 35.

Travel south on Highway 35 for 25 miles to the Polallie picnic area and Elk Meadows trailhead.

Drive time from Portland:
1 hour 30 minutes

Photos, left to right from top: Tamanawas Falls; Cold Spring Creek, mossy boulders; Cold Spring Creek.

TAMANAWAS FALLS

Photos, left to right from top: Cold Spring Creek; trail along a ridge; paintbrush wildflowers; view of the East Fork Hood River; footbridge over Cold Spring Creek.

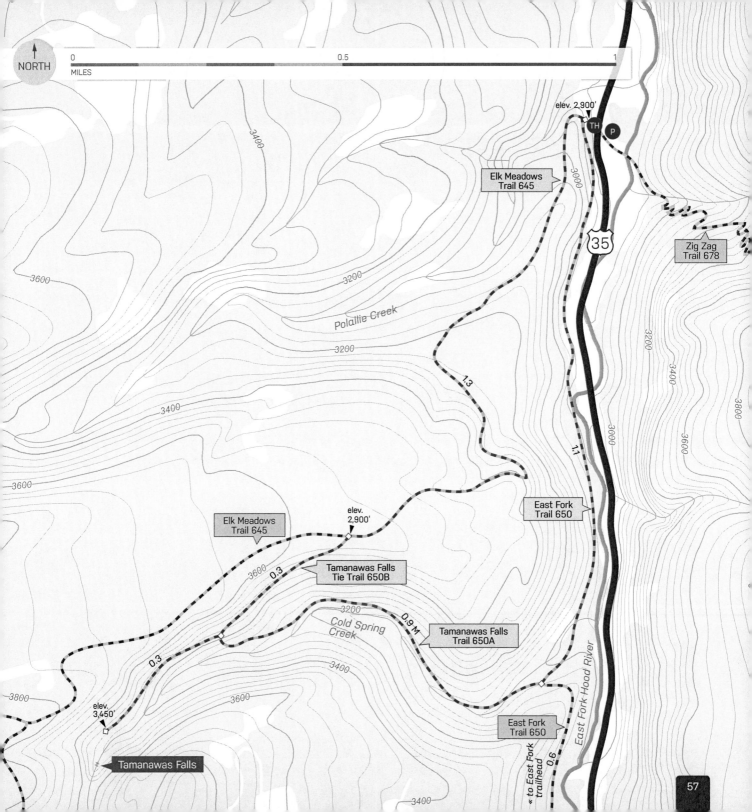

NORTH

MILES
0   0.5   1

elev. 2,900'

TH P

Elk Meadows
Trail 645

3400

3200

Polallie Creek

3200

3600

3400

3600

3600

Zig Zag
Trail 678

35

3200

3400

3600

3800

3000

1.3

1.1

East Fork
Trail 650

Elk Meadows
Trail 645

elev.
2,900'

3600

0.3

Tamanawas Falls
Tie Trail 650B

3200

Cold Spring
Creek

0.9 M

Tamanawas Falls
Trail 650A

3400

0.3

3600

elev.
3,450'

East Fork
Trail 650

East Fork Hood River

0.6

« to East Fork
trailhead

Tamanawas Falls

3400

Salmon River Canyon

Hike beside the Salmon River through a mossy forest with old-growth cedar and fir, primitive campsites, and spring wildflowers to a canyon viewpoint above the river.

DISTANCE: 7.2 miles (roundtrip)

ELEVATION GAIN: 950 ft.

DIFFICULTY: moderate

HIKE TYPE: out and back

TRAIL: packed dirt

OPEN: all year, depending on snow levels

BEST TIME OF YEAR: May - Oct.

FEATURES: river, forest, canyon views, wildflowers

FEES/PERMITS: Northwest Forest Pass required

AGENCY: Zig Zag Ranger District, Mount Hood National Forest

The Salmon River is a designated Wild and Scenic River, all the way from its beginnings at the Palmer snowfield on Mount Hood to where it joins the Sandy River near Brightwood 33 miles later.

Begin this hike at the trailhead located right before a bridge going over the Salmon River. The first two miles of the hike are relatively flat, skirting above the river bank several times, and meandering through an old-growth forest of Douglas fir, western red cedar, and western hemlock. Fallen trees become "nurse" logs, giving life to the moss, ferns, and young trees growing from them. Moss and lichens hang from the trees and cover interesting rocky structures. In late April and early May, spring wildflowers are abundant, including fawn lilies, oxalis, chocolate lilies, yellow violets and fairy slippers. The forest floor is covered with oxalis, changing to Oregon grape and salal as you climb up before reaching a rocky meadow.

Along the way, you'll cross two sturdy footbridges made of stripped logs, the second crossing a picturesque creek that cascades over mossy rocks before meeting the Salmon River. About 1.5 miles in is Rolling Riffle Camp, a small area of rustic camping spots between the trail and the river.

A checkpoint for the Salmon-Huckleberry Wilderness is about 2 miles in. Fill out this free permit and attach to your backpack. Shortly after, the trail begins to climb, sometimes steeply, and swings in away from the river to cross several small drainage areas.

Once you climb out of the forested section, bear to the right and stay on the narrow, rocky trail to a spectacular canyon overlook. The river is about 600 feet below, and you can hear the roar of several unseen waterfalls. There are steep scramble paths below, but the rocky slopes are very slippery, and people have fallen off and died while attempting this, so stay on the main trail.

Look for wildflowers in this exposed rocky area, including Indian paintbrush. After the canyon overlook, the trail is much steeper, so this is a good place to turn around and head back the same way.

DIRECTIONS TO TRAILHEAD

From Portland, drive east on Highway 26 for 40 miles to the town of Welches.

One mile past the Welches shopping center, turn right on Salmon River Road.

Continue on the Salmon River Road for 5 miles, passing several trailheads for the Old Salmon River Trail.

Trailhead parking is on both sides of the road, just before a bridge crossing the Salmon River.

DRIVE TIME FROM PORTLAND
1 hour 15 minutes

Photos, left to right from top: Salmon River; mossy rock section; old-growth forest; bridge over a creek; view from the bridge.

SALMON RIVER CANYON

Photos, left to right from top: view of the Salmon River Canyon from the trail; avalanche lilies in May; chocolate lilies; Salmon River; old-growth forest.

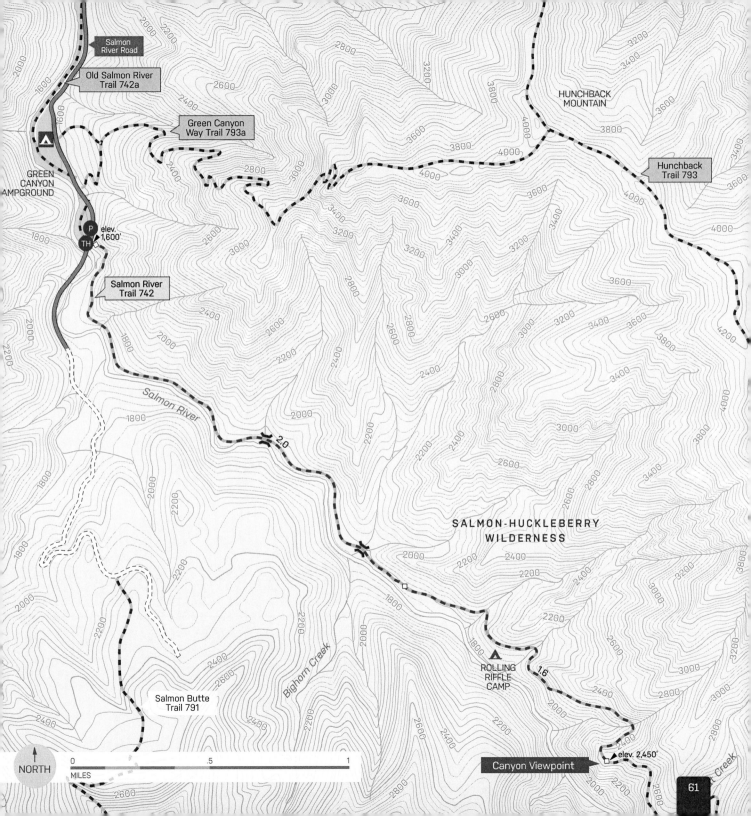

Salmon
River Road

Old Salmon River
Trail 742a

Green Canyon
Way Trail 793a

HUNCHBACK
MOUNTAIN

Hunchback
Trail 793

GREEN
CANYON
CAMPGROUND

P elev.
1,600'
TH

Salmon River
Trail 742

Salmon River

2.0

SALMON-HUCKLEBERRY
WILDERNESS

Bighorn Creek

ROLLING
RIFFLE
CAMP

1.6

Salmon Butte
Trail 791

NORTH

0   .5   1

MILES

Canyon Viewpoint   elev. 2,450'

Oregon
Coast

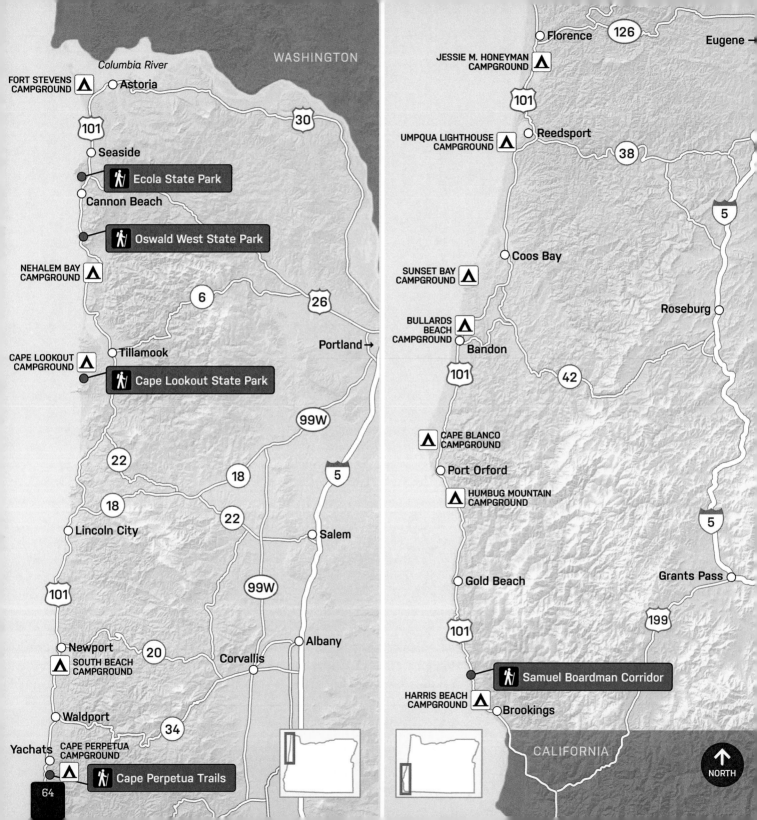

WASHINGTON

Columbia River

FORT STEVENS CAMPGROUND Astoria

101

Seaside

🥾 Ecola State Park

Cannon Beach

🥾 Oswald West State Park

NEHALEM BAY CAMPGROUND

6

26

30

Portland →

CAPE LOOKOUT CAMPGROUND Tillamook

🥾 Cape Lookout State Park

99W

22

18

18

22

99W

Lincoln City

Salem

101

20

Newport

SOUTH BEACH CAMPGROUND

Corvallis

Albany

Waldport

34

Yachats

CAPE PERPETUA CAMPGROUND

🥾 Cape Perpetua Trails

64

Florence 126 Eugene →

JESSIE M. HONEYMAN CAMPGROUND

101

UMPQUA LIGHTHOUSE CAMPGROUND Reedsport

38

5

Coos Bay

SUNSET BAY CAMPGROUND

Roseburg

BULLARDS BEACH CAMPGROUND

Bandon

101

42

CAPE BLANCO CAMPGROUND

Port Orford

5

HUMBUG MOUNTAIN CAMPGROUND

Gold Beach

Grants Pass

199

101

🥾 Samuel Boardman Corridor

HARRIS BEACH CAMPGROUND Brookings

CALIFORNIA

⬆ NORTH

A dramatic landscape where the forest and mountains meet the sea, the Oregon coast is lined with beaches, volcanic headlands and sea stacks, and backed by the Coastal Mountain Range.

The general public was forever given free access to the entire 363-mile Oregon coastline in the state's landmark 1967 Beach Bill. And that access is made easier by Highway 101, which runs parallel to the coastline, at times twisting and turning right next to the shore. Hikes along the coast include trails up to mountain summits, along capes, across headlands, and on beaches.

The North Coast includes scenic Ecola State Park near the arty community of Cannon Beach and Cape Lookout State Park near the town of Tillamook, famous for it's cheese and ice cream company of the same name. Some of the largest remaining tracts of old-growth coastal forest are found along the Central Coast's Cape Perpetua Scenic Area, with plenty of trails to explore them. The Southern Oregon Coast is more remote and isolated, and features the Oregon Dunes near the town of Florence and the some of the coast's most scenic vistas along the Samuel Boardman Scenic Corridor.

Coast Range temperate rain forests are filled with Sitka spruce, western hemlock, western red cedar, and Douglas fir, while the understory is often completely covered in ferns and salal. The coast receives 60-80 inches of rain each year, most of which falls from October to May. Due to this, the forests are mossy and green all year long.

Tidepools at the Oregon Coast: sea anenome; starfish; mussels and barnacles.

Take one of three hikes at Ecola State Park – one of the most scenic sections along the Oregon Coast – to secluded Crescent Beach, to Indian Beach, or follow a route on Tillamook Head taken by Lewis and Clark.

Ecola State Park is located on the north end of Cannon Beach, a charming beach town filled with shops, restaurants, and art galleries. The name Ecola originates from the Chinook tribe's word for whale: "ekoli." Lewis and Clark crossed the headland at Tillamook Head in 1806 to purchase whale blubber from the local tribes at what is now Cannon Beach.

The park was originally developed by the Civilian Conservation Corps and includes two parking areas for beach and hiking trail access. Park at Ecola Point to access the Crescent Beach hike, which is only accessible via the 1.2 mile descent to the secluded beach.

Crescent Beach hike: park at Ecola Point and look for the trailhead near the restrooms. This secluded beach is one of the most photographed places in Oregon. Bounded on the north by Ecola Point and on the south by Chapman Point, this pocket beach is only accessible via the 1.2 mile hike down a steep and often muddy trail, making it more isolated than most beaches on the northern coast.

Ecola Point to Indian Beach hike: park at either Ecola Point or Indian Beach for this 1.5 mile hike along the coastline through old-growth coastal rainforest. The trail is often muddy and after winter storms has a lot of blowdown, so trail conditions sometimes require climbing up and around obstructions. Regardless, the views along this hike are well worth the effort.

Tillamook Head hike: this massive basalt headland and the trail continue all the way to Seaside, Oregon, and were part of the route taken by Lewis and Clark. Like Cape Lookout, Tillamook Head was formed by the massive lava flows 15 million years ago as they spread out over the coastline. About 1.5 miles in is a hikers' camp with three open-sided shelters. A fork in the trail leads to a viewpoint looking out towards Tillamook Lighthouse, which is located more than a mile off the coastline, and passes a World War II bunker built to house radar equipment. For a loop, take the wider "Clatsop Loop" road back to Indian Beach.

BACKPACKING

The hiker camp at Tillamook Head is primarily used by through-hikers doing the Oregon Coast Trail. Access via Indian Beach (1.6 miles to hiker camp) or Seaside (4 miles to hiker camp) trailheads. Overnight parking is not allowed at either trailhead, so you'll need to find an alternative parking spot. There is firewood available for purchase and a vault

---

CRESCENT BEACH
Distance: 2.4 miles (roundtrip)
Elevation gain: 200 ft.
Difficulty: easy to moderate

ECOLA POINT TO INDIAN BEACH
Distance: 3 miles (roundtrip)
Elevation gain: 200 ft.
Difficulty: easy

TILLAMOOK HEAD
Distance: 3.2 miles (roundtrip)
Elevation gain: 800 ft.
Difficulty: moderate

Hike types: out and back
Trails: packed dirt (often muddy)
Best time of year: all year, except during winter storms
Features: coastal forest, ocean views, beaches, whale watching
Fees/permits: Oregon State Parks day use fee
Agency: Oregon State Parks

DRIVING DIRECTIONS

From Portland, drive 74 miles west on Highway 26.

Take the US 101 South exit (Oregon Coast Highway).

Continue for 3 miles to the first exit for Cannon Beach.

Turn right, and just past the stop sign, turn right at a sign for Ecola State Park.

Follow this road for 1.5 miles to the entry booth for day use payment.

Turn left to park at Ecola Point, or continue for another 1.5 miles to the parking area at Indian Beach.

DRIVE TIME FROM PORTLAND
1 hour 30 minutes

Photos, left to right from top:
Crescent Beach; view from Tillamook Head trail; waterfall on Crescent Beach.

ECOLA STATE PARK

Photos, left to right from top: Indian Beach; view from trail to Indian Beach; World War II bunker for radar equipment on Tillamook Head; muddy trail in coastal forest; hiker camp on Tillamook Head.

HIKER
CAMP

viewpoint

elev. 760'

TILLAMOOK
HEAD

Clatsop
Loop Trail

Indian Creek

Canyon Creek

1.6

Tillamook
Head Trail

INDIAN
POINT

TH P

elev. 20'

Indian Beach

Pacific Ocean

1.5

Ecola State
Park Road

Ecola Point to
Indian Beach

P TH

TH

ECOLA
POINT

elev. 200'

Crescent Beach
Trail

1.2

Crescent Beach

Ecola State
Park Road

101

CHAPMAN
POINT

NORTH

0   .5   1

MILES

Oswald West State Park

Oswald West State Park features old-growth coastal rainforest hikes to Short Sand Beach, to the end of Cape Falcon, and to the top of Neahkahnie Mountain.

Cape Falcon & Short Sand Beach: Begin at the parking area marked for Cape Falcon. The trail runs along the side of a forested ridge above Short Sand Creek for a half mile to a junction. To visit Short Sand Beach, turn left. For the Cape Falcon hike, turn right and follow the trail towards the cape.

Beginning in a forest of Sitka spruce, western hemlock, western red cedar, and fir and filled with ferns, the trail goes through wet boggy areas that are usually quite muddy. Frequent coastal storms mean that there can be lots of blowdown on the trail, so climbing around fallen trees and washed out trail is common. In early spring, trilliums and skunk cabbage are in bloom.

As the trail climbs the cape, ocean waves crash below and the forest opens to provide views of the beach. The trail soon descends and crosses a small creek. Look for a side trail on the left that goes to a viewpoint of Blumenthal Falls (45 ft.).

Continue on the main trail along several switchbacks going up to the headland. Native salal on both sides of the trail form a tunnel as you make your way along an often muddy trench between them.

At the top of the headland, take the left spur where the trail divides. There are several open areas along the cliff edge to take in the views all around. To reach the end of the cape, look for an obvious but unsigned trail heading into a shrubby knoll. Work your way through the vegetation to the narrow and rocky cape. Be careful to not get too close to the sheer edges of the cape here. The view to the south includes Neahkahnie Mountain and the beach town of Manzanita, and on clear days, views to the north all the way to Tillamook Head and south to Cape Lookout. Return the same way.

Neahkahnie Mountain hike: Begin at the northern trailhead for Neahkahnie Mountain, directly across Highway 101 from the parking area. The hike begins in forest, then switchbacks up the side of the mountain through a tunnel of thickets of salal and shrubbery. There are views to the west of the ocean, Cape Falcon and Smugglers Cove.

The next section of trail goes through forest, switchbacking several times as it winds its way around the sides of the mountain. Nearing the top, the trail opens suddenly with wide open views of the ocean to the south and a rocky scramble path up to the top. Continue on the trail a short distance, turning to the left for an easier path to the top.

At the rocky summit, take in the views looking south and down towards Manzanita, Nehalem Bay, and on a clear day, all the way to Cape Lookout. Return the same way.

CAPE FALCON
Distance: 5 miles (roundtrip)
Elevation gain: 260 ft.
Difficulty: easy

NEAHKAHNIE MOUNTAIN
Distance: 4 miles (roundtrip)
Elevation gain: 1,450 ft.
Difficulty: moderate

SHORT SAND BEACH
Distance: 1 mile (roundtrip)
Elevation gain: 60 ft.
Difficulty: easy

Hike types: out and back
Trails: packed dirt (often muddy)
Best time of year: all year, except during winter storms
Features: coastal forest, ocean views, beaches, whale watching
Fees/permits: Oregon State Parks day use fee
Agency: Oregon State Parks

DRIVING DIRECTIONS

From Portland, drive 74 miles west on Highway 26.

Take the US 101 South exit (Oregon Coast Highway).

Continue for 14 miles and park in one of the park's three parking areas.

To reach Neahkahnie Mountain's northern trailhead, drive another mile to a pullout on the right side of 101 highway.

DRIVE TIME FROM PORTLAND
1 hour 40 minutes

Photos, left to right from top: view to the south from Neahkahnie Mountain; Cape Falcon; Short Sand Beach; coastal forest with undergrowth of ferns and oxalis.

OSWALD WEST STATE PARK

Photos, left to right from top: view of Cape Falcon and Smuggler's Cove from the Neahkahnie Mountain North Trail; suspension bridge over Necarney Creek; churning water at Cape Falcon; old-growth Sitka Spruce; view of Short Sand Beach through the trees.

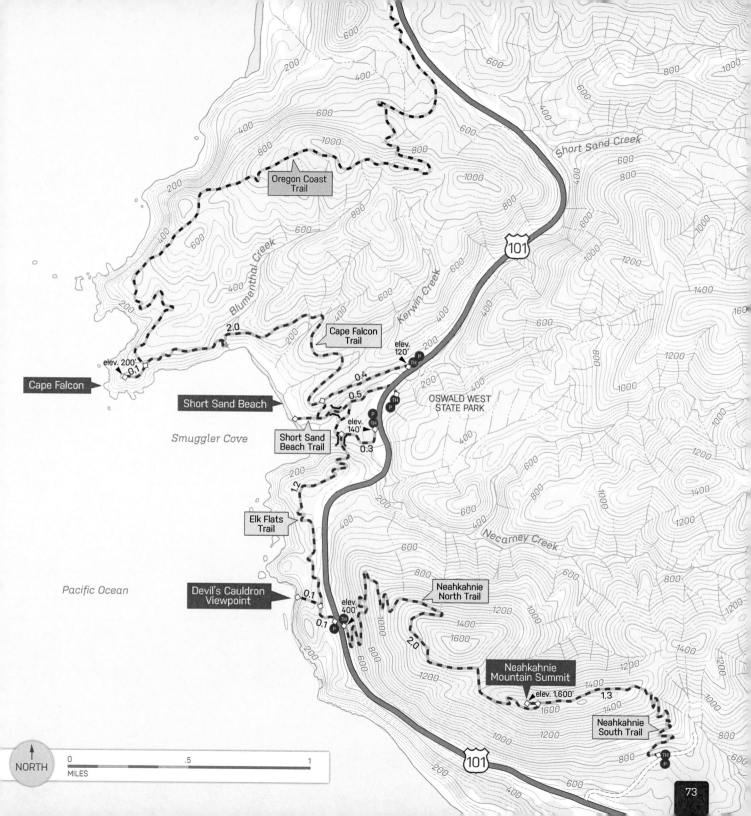

Oregon Coast Trail

Cape Falcon Trail

elev. 120'

Cape Falcon
elev. 200'
0.1
2.0

Short Sand Beach
0.4
0.5

Short Sand Beach Trail
elev. 140'
0.3

Smuggler Cove

OSWALD WEST STATE PARK

Blumenthal Creek

Kerwin Creek

Short Sand Creek

Elk Flats Trail
1.2

Devil's Cauldron Viewpoint
0.1
0.1
elev. 400'

Pacific Ocean

Necarney Creek

Neahkahnie North Trail
2.0

Neahkahnie Mountain Summit
elev. 1,600'
1.3

Neahkahnie South Trail

101

NORTH

0   .5   1
MILES

Cape Lookout State Park

Hike the length of Cape Lookout, a basalt headland with spectacular views 400 feet above the ocean, or on Netarts Spit, a 5-mile long narrow section of beach that separates Netarts Bay from the ocean.

Cape Lookout hike: From the trailhead, take the Cape Trail for a hike to the end of the cape. Since this part of the Oregon coast receives about 100 inches of rain each year, the trail is often wet and muddy. Short sections of the trail have boardwalks, but there are plenty of spots where the mud covers the entire trail.

Cape Lookout was formed 15 million years ago when massive lava floods flowed down the Columbia River and fanned out down the coastline, hardening into basalt headlands.

The dense forest is filled with old-growth Sitka spruce, with an understory of ferns, salal, and salmonberry. Views to the south include a secluded beach accessible via the South Trail junction.

At about .6 miles in, a marker commemorates a World War II B-17 bomber that crashed nearby. At 1.2 miles in, an overlook provides views to the north, showing the waves crashing below at the edge of the cape. Sections of the trail are along open cliffs with 400 feet drop-offs, so be careful to watch your step.

At the end of the cape, views of the ocean stretch out endlessly westward, and to the south toward Cape Kiwanda and Cascade Head.

Gray whales migrate close to shore from December to June, and this is one of the best locations in Oregon to view them as they detour around the cape. Return the same way.

Netarts Spit hike: Begin the hike at Cape Lookout State Park's day use area. Since part of the beach gets cut off during high tides, plan to do this hike at low tide.

Follow an access trail to the beach, and head north for five miles to the end of the spit at the opening of Netarts Bay. Along the beach, the bay is hidden from site by short dunes, but there are several areas along the dune to climb up for a view of the bay and Coastal Mountains behind it.

To the north, the small beach communities of Oceanside and Netarts are visible. About a half-mile off the coastline, Three Arch Rocks National Wildlife Refuge provides protection for more than 150 species of birds, including Oregon's largest breeding colony of tufted puffins.

At the end of the spit where the ocean and the bay meet, the waves change direction, angling towards shore, splashing into small pools of water along the shoreline. At the tip of the cape, harbor seals sometimes gather to sun, and at low tides, the bay's mud flats are a popular spot for clamming. Return the same way.

CAPE LOOKOUT

DISTANCE: 5.2 miles (roundtrip)
ELEVATION GAIN: 450 ft.
DIFFICULTY: easy

NETARTS SPIT

DISTANCE: 10.6 miles (roundtrip)
DIFFICULTY: moderate

HIKE TYPES: out and back
BEST TIME OF YEAR: all year, except during winter storms
FEATURES: ocean views, coastal forest, whale watching
FEES/PERMITS: Oregon State Parks day use fee
AGENCY: Oregon State Parks

DIRECTIONS TO TRAILHEAD

From Portland, drive west for 20 miles on Highway 26 to the Highway 6 exit. Stay to the left and continue on Highway 6 for 50 miles.

At the Highway 101 junction in Tillamook, follow signs for Cape Lookout State Park, continuing straight on 1st St.

Turn left on Birch St., then right on 3rd St., which becomes Netarts Highway.

Continue on Netarts Highway for 4.5 miles.

Following signs for Cape Lookout State Park, turn left at Whiskey Creek Road.

Netarts Spit hike: Continue for about 6 miles to the Cape Lookout State Park entrance, and follow signs to the day use area.

Cape Lookout hike: Continue for about 8 miles to the trailhead parking lot at the top of a hill on the right.

DRIVE TIME FROM PORTLAND
1 hour 45 minutes

Photos, left to right from top: Cape Lookout; view to the south from Cape Lookout trail; Netarts Spit; coastal forest at Cape Lookout trail.

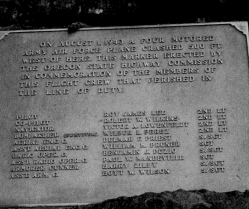

ON AUGUST 1, 1943 A FOUR MOTORED
ARMY AIR FORCE PLANE CRASHED 500 FT.
WEST OF HERE. THIS MARKER ERECTED BY
THE OREGON STATE HIGHWAY COMMISSION
IN COMMEMORATION OF THE MEMBERS OF
THIS FLIGHT CREW THAT PERISHED IN
THE LINE OF DUTY.

PILOT   ROY JAMES LEE   2ND LT
CO-PILOT   ROBERT W. WILKINS   2ND LT
NAVIGATOR   VICTOR A. LOWENFELDT   2ND LT
BOMBARDIER (SURVIVOR)   WILBUR L. PEREZ   2ND LT
AERIAL ENG. G.   DELMAR F. PRIEST   S/SGT
ASS'T AERIAL ENG. G.   WILLIAM R. PRUNER   SGT
RADIO OPER. G.   BENJAMIN J. PUZIO   S/SGT
ASS'T RADIO OPER. G.   PAUL W. GANDEVILLE   S/T
ARMORER GUNNER   HARRY LILLY   S/SGT
ASS'T ARM. G.   BOYT W. WILSON   S/SGT

CAPE LOOKOUT STATE PARK

Photos, left to right from top: Viewpoint for
Netarts Spit and Netarts Bay; at the end of
Cape Lookout; plaque memorializing WWII
aircraft crash; Cape Lookout trail section with
boardwalks; view of Netarts Spit from Cape
Lookout trail.

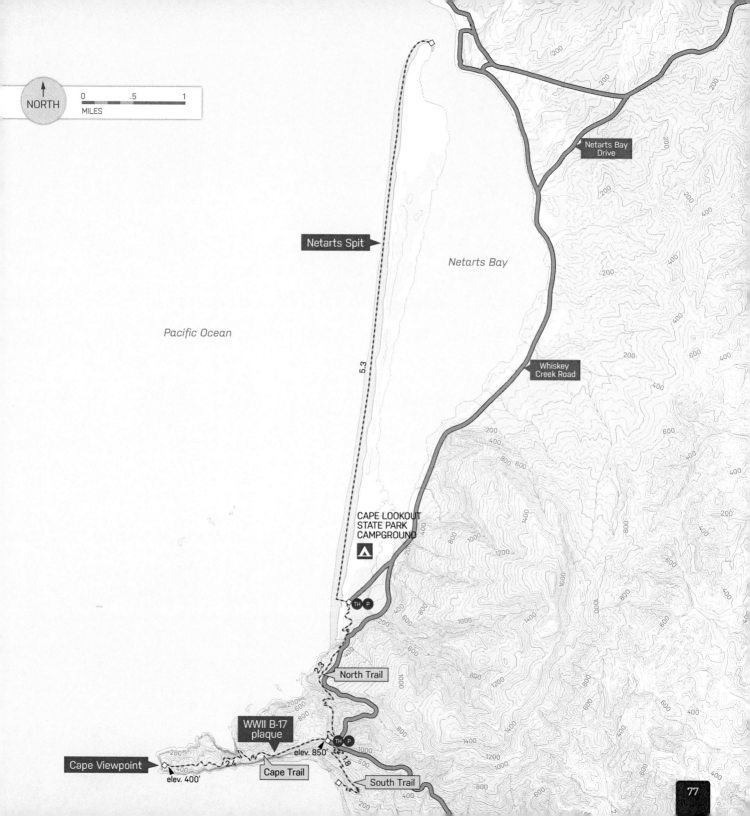

NORTH

0   .5   1
MILES

Pacific Ocean

Netarts Bay

Netarts Spit

5.3

Netarts Bay Drive

Whiskey Creek Road

CAPE LOOKOUT STATE PARK CAMPGROUND

TH P

2.3

North Trail

WWII B-17 plaque

TH P

elev. 850'

1.8

Cape Viewpoint

elev. 400'

2.4

Cape Trail

South Trail

200
400
600
800
1000
1200
1400
1600

Cape Perpetua Scenic Area

The Cape Perpetua Scenic Area has it all: tide pools, churns, spouting horns, old-growth coastal forest, and soaring views of the Oregon coastline.

Located two miles south of Yachats, Oregon (pronounced Yaw-Hots), the Cape Perpetua Scenic Area includes a campground with trails linked to a Visitors Center, so it's easy to spend several days exploring everything this area has to offer. The Visitors Center includes a ranger station, a small gift shop, and interpretive displays about the region's history and ecology. Some of the best remaining old-growth coastal rain forest is accessible via the area's many trails, and a short drive to the top of Cape Perpetua offers outstanding coastline views from this 800 ft.-high promontory.

Captain Cook Trail: From the Visitors Center, take the trail that goes under the highway to reach the rocky coastline. Turn left for Thor's Well, Spouting Horn, and the best tide pooling. Spouting Horn and Thor's Well are best seen at high tide or during winter storms. During a low tide, this area is filled with sea anemones, sea urchins, and other tide pool dwellers.

Restless Waters Trail: From the Visitors Center, take the trail that goes under the highway to reach the rocky coastline. Turn right and continue on this path along the highway for almost a half mile. The trail switchbacks down a hillside next to the ocean. Devil's Churn is the rocky chute at the end of the bluff, with water slamming into the rock and spraying straight up into the air. Best viewed at high tide or during winter storms, make sure to keep your eye on the ocean since sneaker waves can surge in without warning at any time.

Cooks Ridge & Gwynn Creek loop hike: From the Visitors Center, take the trail from the upper parking lot. Begin in a dense forest with Douglas fir and spruce, with a section of old-growth Sitka spruce near a trail junction for the Discovery Loop. Continue on the left trail, gradually ascending the ridge for 1.6 miles to a trail junction. Take the Gwynn Creek trail to the right for the loop hike. The Gwynn Creek trail slowly descends, meandering around several small creeks. A thick undergrowth of ferns lends special beauty to this coastal rain forest. Gwynn Creek is occasionally visible from the trail as you get closer to the coastline. The trail ends at a junction with the Oregon Coast Trail. Take a short detour to the left to a bridge over Gwynn Creek. Turn around and continue on the Oregon Coast Trail all the way to the Visitors Center. With the highway directly below, there are several good views of the ocean through the trees in this section.

CAPTAIN COOK TRAIL
DISTANCE: 0.6 miles (roundtrip)
ELEVATION GAIN: 120 ft.
DIFFICULTY: easy
HIKE TYPE: out and back

RESTLESS WATERS TRAIL
DISTANCE: 1.3 miles (roundtrip)
ELEVATION GAIN: 120 ft.
DIFFICULTY: easy
HIKE TYPE: out and back

COOKS RIDGE & GWYNN CREEK LOOP
DISTANCE: 6.4 miles (roundtrip)
ELEVATION GAIN: 1,200 ft.
DIFFICULTY: moderate
HIKE TYPE: loop

OPEN: all year
BEST TIME OF YEAR: all year
FEATURES: old growth coastal forest
FEES/PERMITS: Northwest Forest Pass required
AGENCY: Siuslaw National Forest

DIRECTIONS TO TRAILHEAD

From Portland, take I-5 South for 9 miles to Exit 294 for 99W Tigard/Newberg.

Continue on 99W for 22.9 miles and turn left onto Highway 18 for Dayton and the Oregon Coast.

Continue on Highway 18 for 53 miles. At a junction with Highway 101 North, stay to the left and merge with Highway 101 South.

Continue on Highway 101 South for 56.5 miles. 3 miles past the town of Yachats, turn left for the Cape Perpetua Visitor Center.

DRIVE TIME FROM PORTLAND
3 hours

Photos, left to right from top: windswept Sitka spruce; waves crashing the rocky shoreline; view from top of Cape Perpetua; seagull; tidepool with sea anemones and purple sea urchins

COOKS RIDGE TRAIL
◊ VISITOR CENTER 2.4
CUMMINS CREEK TRAIL 1.1 ◊
FOREST ROAD NO. 55 1.3 ◊

GWYNN CREEK / COOKS RIDGE LOOP HIKE

Photos, left to right from top: Sitka Spruce; ferns in the forest; Cooks Ridge junction; old-growth tree bark; bridge over Gwynn Creek; dense coastal forest.

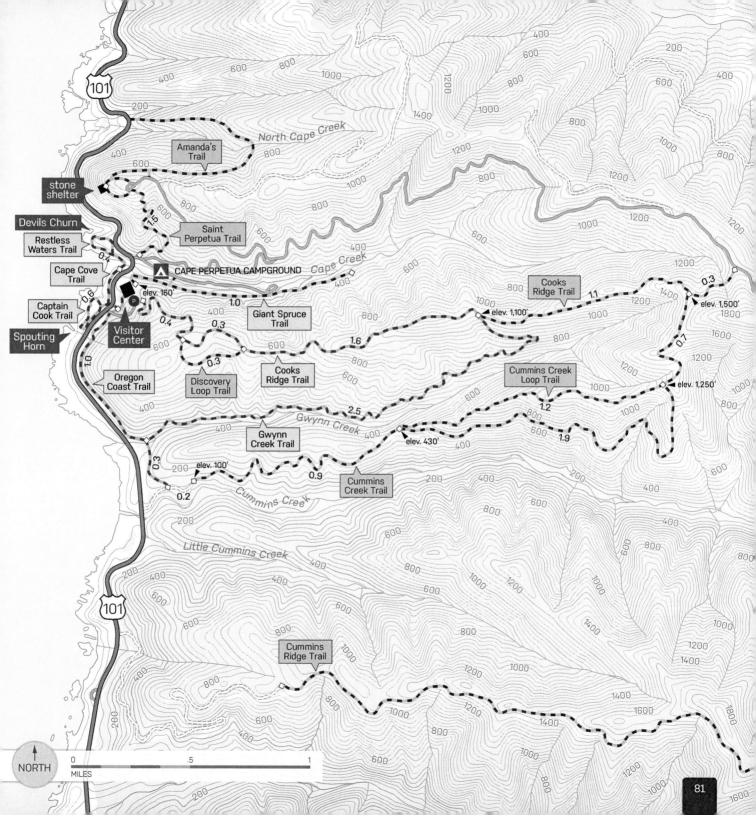

101

400
600
200
400
600
800
1000
1200
1400
800
1000
600
400
200

North Cape Creek

Amanda's Trail

800
600
800
1200
1000
800
1000
1200

stone shelter

1.5

800
600

Saint Perpetua Trail

400

600

1200

1200

Devils Churn

Restless Waters Trail

0.4

Cape Cove Trail

CAPE PERPETUA CAMPGROUND

Cape Creek

600

400

Cooks Ridge Trail

1.1

0.3

elev. 1,500'

1800

Captain Cook Trail

0.6

elev. 160'

1.0

Giant Spruce Trail

400

800

1000

elev. 1,100'

1200

1400

1000

1600

1200

Spouting Horn

Visitor Center

0.4

0.3

600

Cooks Ridge Trail

1.6

600

800

600

800

1000

0.7

1200

Cummins Creek Loop Trail

1.2

elev. 1,250'

1000

800

Oregon Coast Trail

1.0

0.3

Discovery Loop Trail

400

2.5

Gwynn Creek

Gwynn Creek Trail

400

1.9

600

400

800

600

400

elev. 430'

200

400

600

0.3

200

elev. 100'

0.9

Cummins Creek Trail

200

400

600

800

1000

0.2

Cummins Creek

600

800

400

Little Cummins Creek

400

200

200

400

600

800

1000

1200

1400

1000

800

101

600

800

1000

1200

1000

800

1200

1400

1600

Cummins Ridge Trail

800

1000

600

1200

1400

1600

1800

1000

800

400

600

200

NORTH

0   .5   1
MILES

81

Samuel H. Boardman Scenic Corridor

The Samuel H. Boardman Scenic Corridor is a visually striking and secluded section of Oregon's coast, with jagged cliffs, secluded beaches, and rocky islands.

Located between Brookings and Gold Beach along Highway 101, the Samuel H. Boardman State Scenic Corridor is 12 miles long with numerous pullouts designed to help explore the area.

The Oregon Coast Trail runs the length of the corridor, with 27 miles of trails meandering through coastal forests that feature 300 year-old Sitka spruce. The trail is broken into segments that go through forest, across beaches, and along sections of the highway. The trails here can be confusing, so look for posts with the Oregon Coast Trail marker.

Arch Rock Picnic Area: milepost 344.8
A short paved loop leads to views of Arch Rock at the end of the walkway.

Spruce Island: milepost 345.0
This pullout includes a view of a large island topped with Sitka spruce. Take the trail south for 0.9 miles to a rough and steep side trail leading to Secret Beach.

Thunder Rock Cove: milepost 345.8
One of the most scenic sections of the corridor, a one-mile loop trail leads to a partially wooded grassy headland with fantastic views of rocky islands, cliffs, and secluded beaches.

Natural Bridges: milepost 346.0
A short path leads to a viewpoint of the open arches in the rock formations that make up the natural bridges.

North Island: milepost 347.4
A trail here leads for 0.7 miles down to the black sands of China Beach. The trail is steep and overgrown in places, with a drop of about 350 feet before reaching the beach.

Thomas Creek Bridge: milepost 347.8
Take the trail on the north side of the bridge for a view of Oregon's highest bridge (345 ft.) and the creek far below.

Indian Sands: milepost 348.6
With sculpted sandstone formations and dunes, wildflower meadows and a basalt sea arch, Indian Sands is a unique section in the Boardman Corridor. A steep trail drops 200 feet to a junction with a side trail to the dunes (go right on the side trail, then left at a large opening to reach the dunes).

Whaleshead Picnic Area: milepost 349.1
At a mile long, Whaleshead Beach is the longest beach in this area.

Whaleshead Viewpoint: milepost 349.3
View Whaleshead Beach from above.

House Rock Viewpoint: milepost 351.2
A short trail leads to a viewpoint of the coast, with a monument to the park's founder, Samuel H. Boardman.

Cape Ferrelo Viewpoint: milepost 351.9
Take a one mile loop trail through the open grassy headland of Cape Ferrelo for whale watching, spring wildflowers, and viewing sunsets. For a longer hike, take the trail north for four miles to House Rock Viewpoint. Side trails lead to secluded beaches.

Lone Ranch Picnic Area: milepost 352.6
Lone Ranch Beach has several close to shore sea stacks and is easily accessed via a short path from a parking lot.

DISTANCE: varies for each section
DIFFICULTY: easy to moderate
OPEN: all year
BEST TIME OF YEAR: all year
FEATURES: beaches, old growth forest, ocean vistas
FEES/PERMITS: none needed
AGENCY: Oregon State Parks

DIRECTIONS TO TRAILHEAD

From Portland, take I-5 South for 138 miles to Exit 162 for Highway 38 to Drain /Elkton.

Continue on Highway 38 for 6.3 miles. In the town of Drain, turn right to continue on Highway 38.

Continue for another 50 miles on Highway 38 to Reedsport.

In Reedsport, turn left on Highway 101 South.

Continue on Highway 101 South for 121 miles to the Arch Rock Viewpoint.

DRIVE TIME FROM PORTLAND
6 hours

Photos, left to right from top: Thunder Rock Cove; Natural Bridges Viewpoint; Secret Beach; Indian Sands; China Beach

SAMUEL H. BOARDMAN SCENIC CORRIDOR

Photos, left to right from top: Arch Rock Viewpoint, looking south; Indian Sands; rock islands at Thunder Rock Cove; coastal forest; view to the north from Arch Rock Viewpoint.

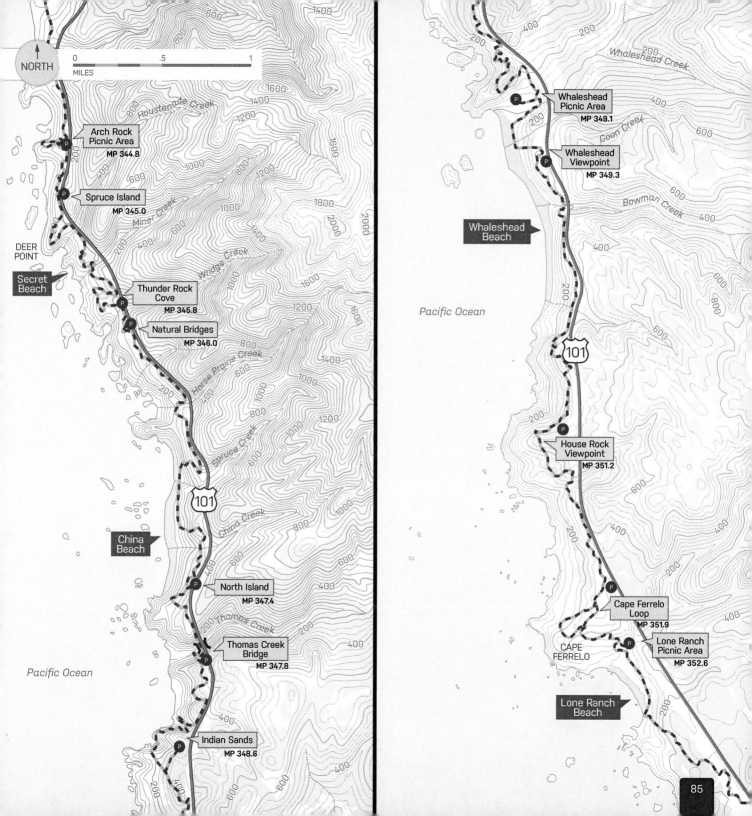

NORTH

0 .5 1
MILES

Arch Rock
Picnic Area
MP 344.8

Spruce Island
MP 345.0

DEER
POINT

Secret
Beach

Thunder Rock
Cove
MP 345.8

Natural Bridges
MP 346.0

China
Beach

North Island
MP 347.4

Thomas Creek
Bridge
MP 347.8

Pacific Ocean

Indian Sands
MP 348.6

Houstenade Creek

Miner Creek

Widge Creek

Horse Prairie Creek

Spruce Creek

China Creek

Thomas Creek

US 101

Whaleshead
Picnic Area
MP 349.1

Whaleshead
Viewpoint
MP 349.3

Whaleshead
Beach

Pacific Ocean

101

House Rock
Viewpoint
MP 351.2

Cape Ferrelo
Loop
MP 351.9

CAPE
FERRELO

Lone Ranch
Picnic Area
MP 352.6

Lone Ranch
Beach

Whaleshead Creek

Coon Creek

Bowman Creek

Painted Hills

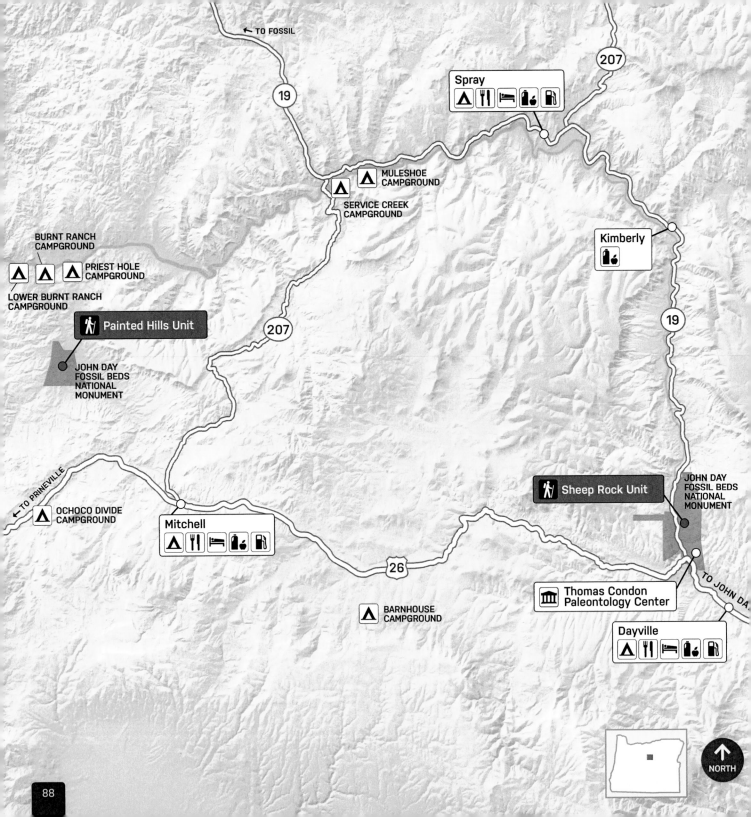

← TO FOSSIL

19

Spray
⛺ 🍴 🛏 🛒 ⛽

207

MULESHOE
CAMPGROUND

SERVICE CREEK
CAMPGROUND

Kimberly
🛒

BURNT RANCH
CAMPGROUND

PRIEST HOLE
CAMPGROUND

LOWER BURNT RANCH
CAMPGROUND

🥾 Painted Hills Unit

JOHN DAY
FOSSIL BEDS
NATIONAL
MONUMENT

207

19

← TO PRINEVILLE

OCHOCO DIVIDE
CAMPGROUND

Mitchell
⛺ 🍴 🛏 🛒 ⛽

26

🥾 Sheep Rock Unit

JOHN DAY
FOSSIL BEDS
NATIONAL
MONUMENT

TO JOHN DA

🏛 Thomas Condon
Paleontology Center

BARNHOUSE
CAMPGROUND

Dayville
⛺ 🍴 🛏 🛒 ⛽

NORTH

The Painted Hills are located in northeastern Oregon's John Day National Fossil Beds Monument, home to over 40 million years' worth of fossils, providing vast insight into the Age of Mammals.

The National Monument covers over 14,000 acres, divided into three separate areas: the Painted Hills Unit, the Sheep Rock Unit, and the Clarno Unit. This book covers the first two.

The Painted Hills Unit is mostly known for its colorful landscape, with rounded hills of claystone in hues of yellows and reds. The Sheep Rock Unit is also known for its geological formations, but here they are blue-green and seemingly carved out of the surrounding hillsides. In all areas of the National Monument, digging or collecting of fossils is strictly prohibited.

The region's climate is semi-arid desert, with only 9-16 inches of annual rainfall — mostly falling in the winter. Spring is a good time to visit, before the extreme heat of the desert summer kicks in. Wildflowers bloom in May, covering portions of the mounds in the Painted Hills. Cacti, sagebrush, and juniper trees are scattered across the landscape's hillsides, grassy areas and rocky terrain. Elevation in the region ranges from 2,000 to 4,500 feet.

Learn more about this area's rich history at the Thomas Condon Paleontology Center, located in the Sheep Rock Unit.

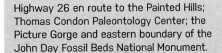

Highway 26 en route to the Painted Hills; Thomas Condon Paleontology Center; the Picture Gorge and eastern boundary of the John Day Fossil Beds National Monument.

Painted Hills Unit Trails

The Painted Hills, with their rounded shapes and bands of color, are truly a natural wonder. Made of layers of heavily eroded volcanic ash, the colors in the exposed tuffs and claystones vary in differing light and moisture conditions.

While none of the trails in the Painted Hills Unit are long enough to feel like a true hike, each highlights different scenery to be found in this unique area. There is no visitor's center here, but there are restrooms and picnic tables. Driving up from 26 highway, you start to see glimpses of the unusual color patterns exposed in the surrounding hillsides, which hint at what is to come – a startling revelation of shape and color. This open, expansive area contains the largest concentration of these uniquely painted ridges and mounds.

For the best views, park at the large gravel lot at the top of a hill and go on the Overlook Trail, an easy half-mile walk up a ridge, with benches at several points for taking in the surrounding scenery. Interpretive displays provide information on how the hills were formed. Additional trails in the park include the Painted Cove, with a boardwalk that takes you between several smaller yet brightly colored mounds, offering close-up views of the claystone in shades from darker red to light purple and yellow. The Carroll Rim Trail climbs 400 feet to panoramic views, and the Red Scar Knoll Trail is the newest – a mostly level trail that ends at a bright yellow and red knoll. The Leaf Hill Trail has interpretive displays highlighting some of the extensive paleontological research that shows some of the leaves found there. Walking off trail in the Painted Hills is prohibited, so please stay on the trails to help protect this fragile environment.

Most of the hills are a tannish to mustard yellow color, with bands of red and streaks of black running through them. Late afternoon provides the best light for photos of the hills. In the spring, yellow cleomes cover parts of the hills and and yellow and purple wildflowers grow in the drainage areas.

The Painted Hills were formed over 35 million years ago as a result of many volcanic eruptions and changes in the climate. This area was once a tropical forest and ancient river floodplain, with prehistoric mammals that are distant relatives to rhinos, tigers, horses and bears. Over time, the landscape changed to the semi-arid desert that it is now, and the ash and soils mixed with minerals and plant material eroded, creating the Painted Hills.

Photos, left to right from top: view from the Painted Hills Overlook Trail; boardwalk through the Painted Cove Trail; rounded shapes of the Painted Hills

---

PAINTED HILLS OVERLOOK
Distance: 0.5 miles (roundtrip)
Elevation gain: 100 ft.

CARROLL RIM TRAIL
Distance: 1.6 miles (roundtrip)
Elevation gain: 400 ft.

PAINTED COVE TRAIL
Distance: 0.25 miles (roundtrip)

RED SCAR KNOLL TRAIL
Distance: 0.25 miles (roundtrip)

LEAF HILL TRAIL
Distance: 0.25 miles (roundtrip)

Difficulty: easy
Trails: rock, dirt, boardwalks
Best time of year: April - June
Features: geological formations
Fees/permits: none
Agency: National Park Service

DIRECTIONS TO TRAILHEAD

From Portland, take I-84 East for 13 miles to Exit 16 for 238th Drive Wood Village.

Turn right on 238th Drive and continue for 3 miles to Burnside.

Turn left onto Burnside and continue for 0.7 miles to the intersection with the Mount Hood Highway 26.

Continue on Highway 26 East for 103 miles to Madras, Oregon.

Just past the town of Madras, turn left to continue on Highway 26 East, continuing for 70.5 miles to Burnt Ranch Road.

Turn left on Burnt Ranch Road and continue for 5.6 miles to Bear Creek Road. Turn left on Bear Creek Road to the parking area for the Painted Hills Overlook.

DRIVE TIME FROM PORTLAND
4 hours

PAINTED HILLS UNIT TRAILS

Photos, left to right from top: view to the north from Painted Hills Overlook Trail; ridges surrounding the Painted Hills; close-up of clay texture; varied colors of the Painted Cove Trail; boardwalk through the Painted Cove Trail

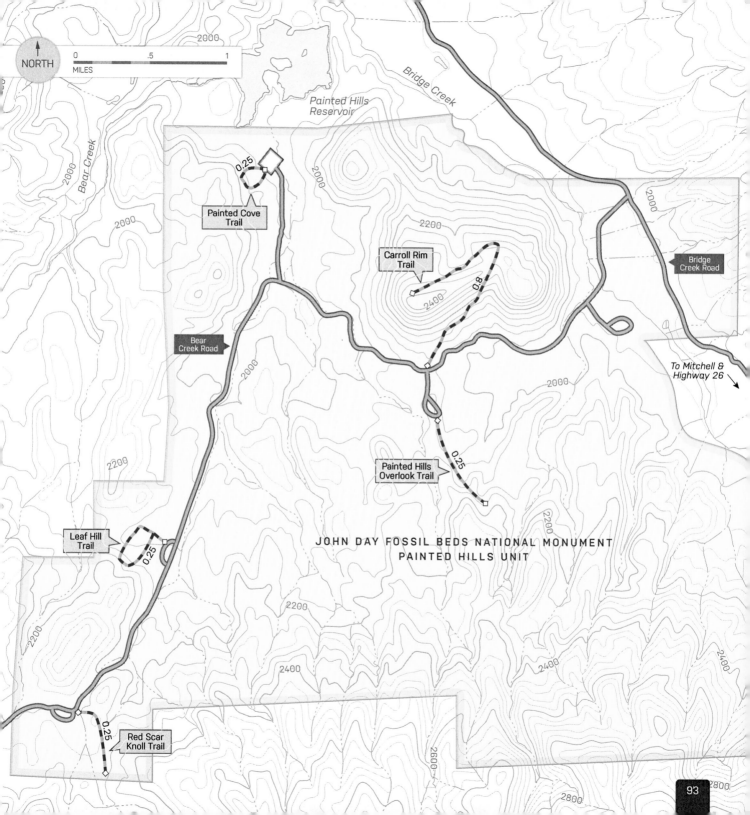

NORTH

MILES
0 .5 1

2000

Bear Creek

Painted Hills
Reservoir

Bridge Creek

2000

2000

2000

2000

0.25

Painted Cove
Trail

2200

Carroll Rim
Trail

0.8

2400

Bridge
Creek Road

2000

Bear Creek
Road

2000

To Mitchell &
Highway 26

2000

0.25

Painted Hills
Overlook Trail

2200

Leaf Hill
Trail

0.25

JOHN DAY FOSSIL BEDS NATIONAL MONUMENT
PAINTED HILLS UNIT

2200

2200

2200

2200

2400

2400

2400

2600

0.25

Red Scar
Knoll Trail

2800

Blue Basin + Island in Time Trails

While the Sheep Rock unit has several trails for hiking, the Blue Basin Trail is the longest option, with up-close views of unusual blue-green formations exposed in the hillsides.

Blue Basin Trail: The Blue Basin hike is best done in a clockwise direction, beginning next to the trailhead sign. The first section of the trail is flat, looping around the hills and providing the first glimpses of minty blue-green formations exposed in the hillsides, sharply contrasting with the surrounding landscape. The greenish chalky hue even colors the water in a small outlet stream.

Juniper trees and sage shrubs dot the hills as you begin the hike up a narrow canyon. A boardwalk section near the top leads to a bench and panoramic views of the John Day Basin, with the John Day river winding its way through green fields.

At the top of the basin, the trail rounds the sloping hills, with a side trail to an overlook with more views. Continuing on the main trail, a short section goes through private land divided with fencing and gates to walk through. Back on national monument land, switchbacks eventually lead back to the trailhead.

Island in Time Trail: Just before the Blue Basin loop ends, the Island in Time Trail crosses the trail to the right. This trail takes you into the heart of the other-worldly blue-green formations. There are 13 grated-surface bridges along this trail, making it difficult on a dog's paws, so it's recommended to not take dogs unless you can carry them across the bridges. Winding through the heaviest concentration of these blue-green formations, with interpretive panels and replicas of fossils spaced throughout, you are completely surrounded by this surreal landscape at the end of the trail.

While in the Sheep Rock Unit, a stop at the Thomas Condon Paleontology Center is highly recommended. The center houses interpretive displays about the history of the area, a small gift shop, and a ranger station. Sheep Rock dominates the views around the center, towering over the surrounding hills.

This area is home to a vast number of unique fossils that span 40 million years and provide unparalleled records of the Age of Mammals not found elsewhere in the world. A noted paleontologist, Dr. Ralph W. Chaney stated "No region in the world shows a more complete sequence of Tertiary land populations, both plant and animal, than the John Day Basin."

Photos, left to right from top: expansive views of the John Day Basin; formations along the Blue Basin Trail; looking into the Blue Basin; view from the top of the trail; Islands in Time Trail.

BLUE BASIN TRAIL

DISTANCE: 3.25 miles (roundtrip)

ELEVATION GAIN: 600 ft.

DIFFICULTY: easy to moderate

ISLAND IN TIME TRAIL

DISTANCE: 1.3 miles (roundtrip)

DIFFICULTY: easy

NOTE: this trail includes 13 bridges with grated surfaces and is not recommended for dogs

---

TOTAL DISTANCE FOR BOTH TRAILS: 4.1 miles (roundtrip)

HIKE TYPE: loop

BEST TIME OF YEAR: April - June

FEATURES: geological features, panoramic views

FEES/PERMITS: none

AGENCY: National Park Service

DIRECTIONS TO TRAILHEAD

From Portland, take I-84 East for 13 miles to Exit 16 for 238th Drive Wood Village.

Turn right on 238th Drive and continue for 3 miles to Burnside.

Turn left onto Burnside and continue for 0.7 miles to the intersection with the Mount Hood Highway 26.

Continue on Highway 26 East for 103 miles to Madras, Oregon.

Just past the town of Madras, turn left to continue on Highway 26 East, continuing for 105 miles to Highway 19 North.

Turn left on Highway 19 and continue for 5 miles to the trailhead for the Blue Basin Trail (on the right).

DRIVE TIME FROM PORTLAND 4 hours 30 minutes

BLUE BASIN + ISLAND IN TIME TRAILS

Photos, left to right from top: Blue Basin Trail; close-up of the formations; old Juniper tree; exposed hillsides; Islands in Time Trail.

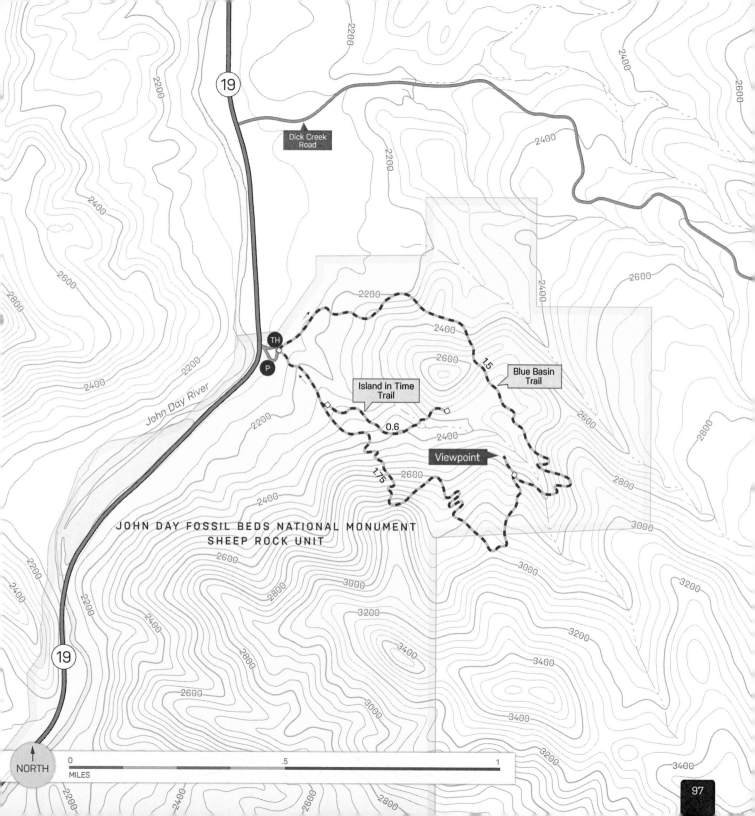

19

Dick Creek
Road

2200
2200
2400
2400
2600
2600

TH
P

John Day River

Island in Time
Trail

Blue Basin
Trail

1.5

0.6

Viewpoint

1.75

JOHN DAY FOSSIL BEDS NATIONAL MONUMENT
SHEEP ROCK UNIT

19

NORTH

| 0 | | .5 | | 1 |
MILES

Smith Rock

TO MADRAS →

Misery Ridge Trail

River Trail

SMITH ROCK
STATE PARK

SMITH ROCK
BIVOUAC CAMPGROUND

Terrebonne

97

← TO REDMOND

NORTH

Smith Rock State Park is located in the high desert of Central Oregon. An internationally renowned location for rock climbing, the park also has plenty of trails for hikers who want to experience the majestic rock scenery.

The Crooked River winds through the park, creating a picturesque and completely unique setting for some of the best rock climbing in America and a few outstanding hikes as well. The park has many miles of trails that provide hikers with striking views of the river, the rock formations, and the surrounding landscape.

Like so many Pacific Northwest landscapes, these sheer cliffs of tuff and basalt were formed by volcanic activity, dating back about 30 million years. Eventually, the Crooked River cut its way through the rock to create the river canyon we have today, which rests beneath jagged, reddish colored rocks that tower some 800 feet above the pristine river at their base.

There's no mistaking that this is the high desert, because the landscape is one of sagebrush and Ponderosa pine, and the summers can be quite hot. For heat lovers, summer may be the best time to visit, but for those who prefer cooler weather, spring and autumn bring a more temperate climate to this rugged wonder, when the sun is still bright, but the air is cooler and wildlife is more abundant... or at least more apparent.

Smith Rock State Park provides a day-use area that's open year-round and includes a visitor center, restrooms, and picnic facilities. There's also a tent-only campground, which offers outstanding views of the cliffs and valley.

Photos, top to bottom: the park's campground entrance, view from a campsite, climbers making their way up Monkey Face.

River Trail + Misery Ridge

The Misery Ridge and River Trails showcase the best highlights of the park, winding around the rock formations next to the river, and then all the way to the top, with sweeping vistas in all directions.

DISTANCE: 4.6 miles (roundtrip)

ELEVATION GAIN: 1,000 ft.

DIFFICULTY: moderate

HIKE TYPE: loop

TRAIL: packed dirt and loose rock

OPEN: all year

BEST TIME OF YEAR: anytime except July and August

FEATURES: geological features, mountain views, wildlife

FEES/PERMITS: Oregon State Park pass required (paystations at the park)

AGENCY: Oregon State Parks

To avoid the heat of the high desert during the summer months, do this hike early in the day, or visit during the spring or fall. From the main parking lot, take the Rim Rock Trail, winding around the park's east rim with great views into the river canyon before heading back towards the park's visitors center. Past the buildings, take the The Chute Trail into the river canyon. Cross the bridge and turn left on the River Trail – the park's rangers are advising people to hike the loop in this direction instead of heading up the east side of the Misery Ridge Trail directly across from the bridge. The west side is steeper, with a lot of scree (loose rock) on the trail, so it's easier to hike up this section than it is to come down on the way back.

Hiking beside the river as it twists and turns its way through the craggy rocks, this section of trail is close to several popular rock climbing areas, perfect for watching the rock climbers make their way up the sheer rock faces. To get an even closer view, there are many side trails and steps leading up to the routes used by the climbers.

Rounding the southern tip of the park, the trail forks just below Asterisk Pass. At that point, take the Mesa Verde Trail up towards Monkey Face. Passing next to the base of Monkey Face, it is common to see climbers working their way up the face of this dramatic spire.

The next section of trail is Misery Ridge, with steep, scree-covered switchbacks heading all the way to the top. Once at the top, soak in the stunning views of the Cascades, including Mount Jefferson, Three Fingered Jack, Mount Washington, Black Butte, North Sister, Middle Sister, South Sister, Broken Top, and Mount Bachelor.

At the top of Misery Ridge, ancient gnarled juniper trees, small sage shrubs, and wildflowers are scattered across a wide expanse of the rocky ridge. A side trail leads to an up front view of Monkey Face. With plenty of space to spread out, most people spend a bit of time at top to soak in the views before heading back down. Heading down the northeast side of Misery Ridge, the trail has a combination of switchbacks and steep staircases, passing by some of the busier rock climbing sections of the park. Cross the river on the bridge again and head back up The Chute and the Rim Rock Trail to return to the parking lot.

DIRECTIONS TO TRAILHEAD

From Portland, take I-84 East for 13 miles to Exit 16 for 238th Drive Wood Village.

Turn right on 238th Drive and continue for 3 miles to Burnside.

Turn left onto Burnside and continue for 0.7 miles to the intersection with the Mount Hood Highway 26.

Continue on Highway 26 / Highway 97 for 137 miles to Terrebonne, Oregon.

In Terrebonne, turn left at Smith Rock Way and continue for 0.5 miles to Lambert St.

Turn left on Lambert St and continue for 2.5 miles to Crooked River Drive.

Turn left on Crooked River Drive and continue for 0.5 miles to the Smith Rock State Park parking area.

DRIVE TIME FROM PORTLAND
2 hours 50 minutes

Photos, left to right from top: view to the west from the rim; rock climbers; the Crooked River winding through the park.

SMITH ROCK STATE PARK

Photos, left to right from top: views of Mount Bachelor, Broken Top, South Sister, Middle Sister and North Sister from Misery Ridge; rock climber, ancient juniper tree; Monkey Face; Asterisk Pass (small rock that appears to be balanced on the lower ridge).

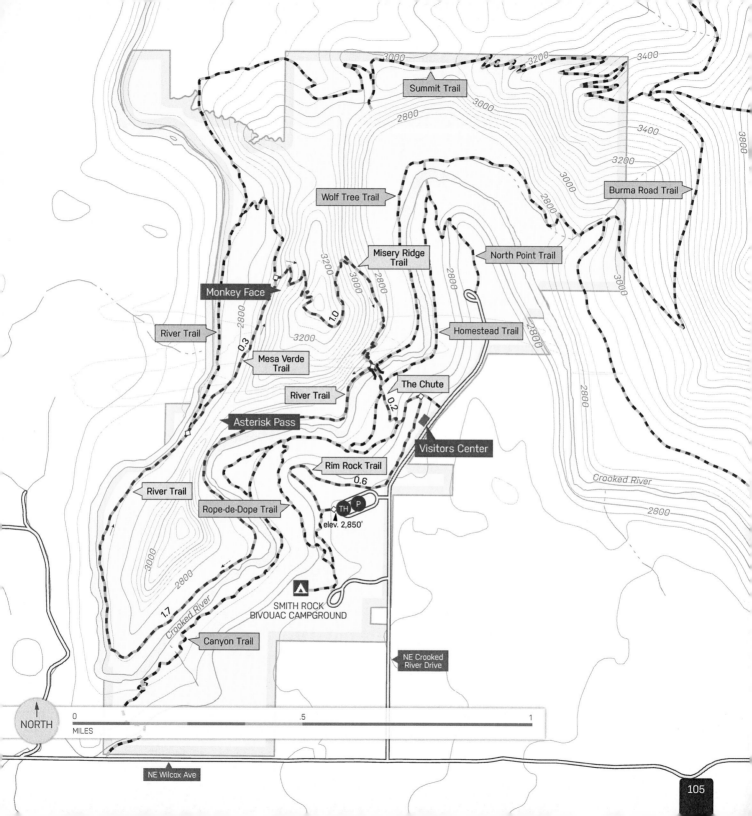

Summit Trail

Wolf Tree Trail

Burma Road Trail

Misery Ridge Trail

North Point Trail

Monkey Face

River Trail

0.3

Homestead Trail

Mesa Verde Trail

River Trail

The Chute

0.2

Asterisk Pass

Visitors Center

Crooked River

Rim Rock Trail

0.6

River Trail

2800

Rope-de-Dope Trail

TH P

elev. 2,850'

1.7

Crooked River

SMITH ROCK
BIVOUAC CAMPGROUND

Canyon Trail

NE Crooked
River Drive

NORTH

0   .5   1

MILES

NE Wilcox Ave

The
Wallowas

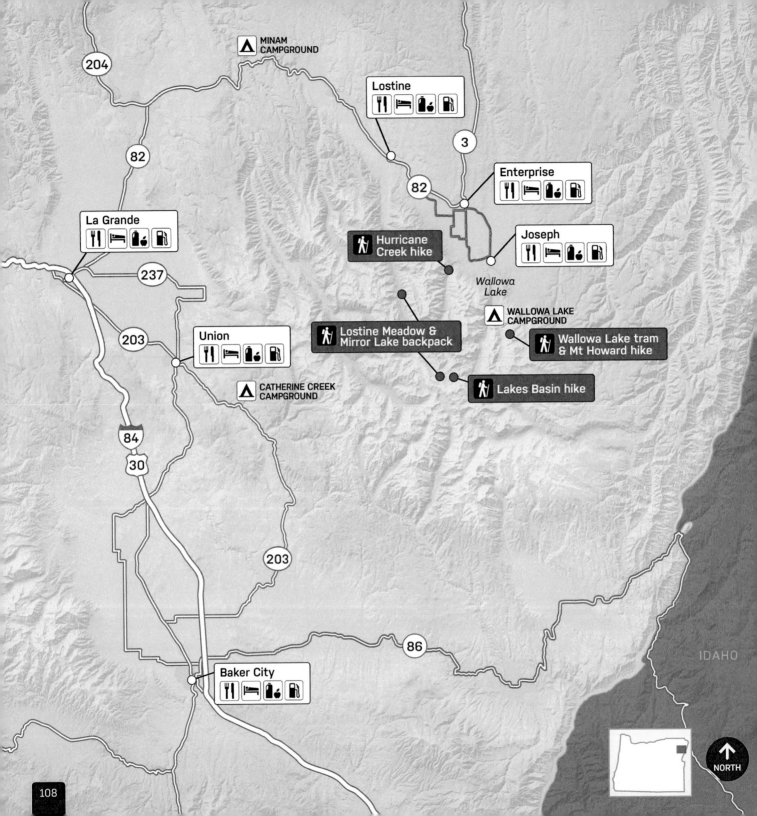

204

MINAM
CAMPGROUND

Lostine
🍴 🛏 🍎 ⛽

3

82

Enterprise
🍴 🛏 🍎 ⛽

La Grande
🍴 🛏 🍎 ⛽

82

Joseph
🍴 🛏 🍎 ⛽

237

🚶 Hurricane
Creek hike

*Wallowa
Lake*

🏕 WALLOWA LAKE
CAMPGROUND

203

Union
🍴 🛏 🍎 ⛽

🚶 Lostine Meadow &
Mirror Lake backpack

🚶 Wallowa Lake tram
& Mt Howard hike

🏕 CATHERINE CREEK
CAMPGROUND

🚶 Lakes Basin hike

84

30

203

86

IDAHO

Baker City
🍴 🛏 🍎 ⛽

NORTH

Known as the "Alps of Oregon," the Wallowa Mountains are located in Northeastern Oregon, with over 360,000 acres designated as the Eagle Cap Wilderness.

The Wallowa (pronounced Wul-OW-wuh) Mountains contain 31 peaks that rise above 9,000 feet, with U-shaped valleys up to a mile below the bare granite peaks and ridges. Alpine lakes and meadows are found throughout higher elevation areas, with granite rock slabs and shelfs scattered all around.

Trees in the area include Ponderosa pine and Douglas fir in lower elevations, transitioning to lodgepole pine, Engelmann spruce and mountain hemlock at mid-elevations, and subalpine fir with whitebark and limber pines at higher elevations.

The area receives 60-75 inches of annual precipitation, with heavy snowfall in the winter. Lower elevation trails are generally accessible in late June and higher elevation trails are usually snow free from mid-July to September. Summer temperatures are often in the 70s and 80s, while night time lows are generally in the 40s, though it can dip below freezing any time of the year.

Chief Joseph and the Nez Perce tribe inhabited this area until the late 1870s, when they were expelled and relocated. Visit the Wallowa Band Nez Perce Trail Interpretive Center in Joseph to learn more about these remarkable indigenous people.

The small town of Joseph, Oregon is filled with galleries, restaurants and interesting shops; Wallowa Lake; the Lostine Tavern restaurant in Lostine, Oregon offers outstanding local food.

Hurricane Creek

This popular day hike to Slick Rock Gorge offers outstanding views of Sacajawea Peak and travels along Hurricane Creek, which flows briskly through a picturesque valley.

The Wallowas are primarily a backpacking destination, with most of the trails covering some distance before opening to views of this spectacular mountain range. But with easy access from the towns of Enterprise and Joseph, the Hurricane Creek trail offers options for both backpacking and day hiking. It stretches for 10.1 miles from the trailhead (5,026') to the Lakes Basin (7,600'), but it also makes for a good out-and-back day hike to Slick Rock Gorge, which is about 3 miles in.

The high walls of Hurwal Divide to the east and Hurricane Divide to the west tower 4,000 feet above the valley floor and Hurricane Creek. A short distance from the trailhead, a side trail leads for 0.2 miles to a viewpoint of Fall Creek Falls (60 ft.). Back on the main trail, cross over Fall Creek and keep following Hurricane Creek. The trail alternates between sections of forest with lodgepole pine, Douglas fir and juniper, to meadows filled with wildflowers in July, including Mariposa lilies, purple penstemon and asters, red paintbrush and yellow cinquefoil.

The highest summit in the Wallowas, Sacajawea Peak (9,838 ft.) dominates the horizon for much of the hike. High ridges connect Sacajawea Peak to white marble-faced Matterhorn, the next highest mountain in the Wallowas.

Hurricane Creek and Divide were originally named by settlers for what they thought were hurricane force winds that severed trees in this area. The trees were instead cut off by avalanches roaring down the steep mountain ridges. Approximately 0.75 miles in is a large section of cut-off trees caused by these avalanches.

Before reaching Slick Rock Gorge, the trail heads away from the creek, switchbacking up the hillside before emerging next to the narrow rocky gorge with the creek chuting through, creating several small waterfalls along the way. At the top of this gorge, Slick Rock Creek cascades down the rocky sides of a high ridge. Cross the creek and continue for a short distance for good views of Hurricane Creek and the gorge. For the day hike, turn around here and return the same way.

For a longer hike or overnight backpacking trip, continue on the trail for another two miles to a side trail that leads steeply up to Echo Lake (8,372 ft.), or continue on to the Lake Basin, 10.1 miles from the trailhead.

DISTANCE: 6.2 miles (roundtrip)

ELEVATION GAIN: 750 ft.

DIFFICULTY: moderate

HIKE TYPE: out and back

TRAIL: packed dirt, rock

OPEN: mid June - Oct.

BEST TIME OF YEAR: July - Sept.

FEATURES: mountain views, waterfalls, wildflowers

FEES/PERMITS: Northwest Forest Pass required

AGENCY: Wallowa-Whitman National Forest; Eagle Cap Wilderness

DIRECTIONS TO TRAILHEAD

From Portland, take I-84 East for 261 miles to Exit 261 Highway 82 / La Grande.

Turn right and continue on Highway 82, following signs for Wallowa Lake for 73 miles to Hurricane Creek Road in the town of Enterprise.

Turn right on Hurricane Creek Road and continue for 8.8 miles to the trailhead.

DRIVE TIME FROM PORTLAND
5 hours 30 minutes

Photos, left to right from top: view of Sacajawea Peak from the trail; Hurricane Creek at Slick Rock Gorge; clear waters of Hurricane Creek.

HURRICANE CREEK

Photos, left to right from top: on the trail above
Slick Rock Gorge; trees damaged by avalanches;
trail sign; waterfall at Slick Rock Gorge;
Hurricane Divide Ridge.

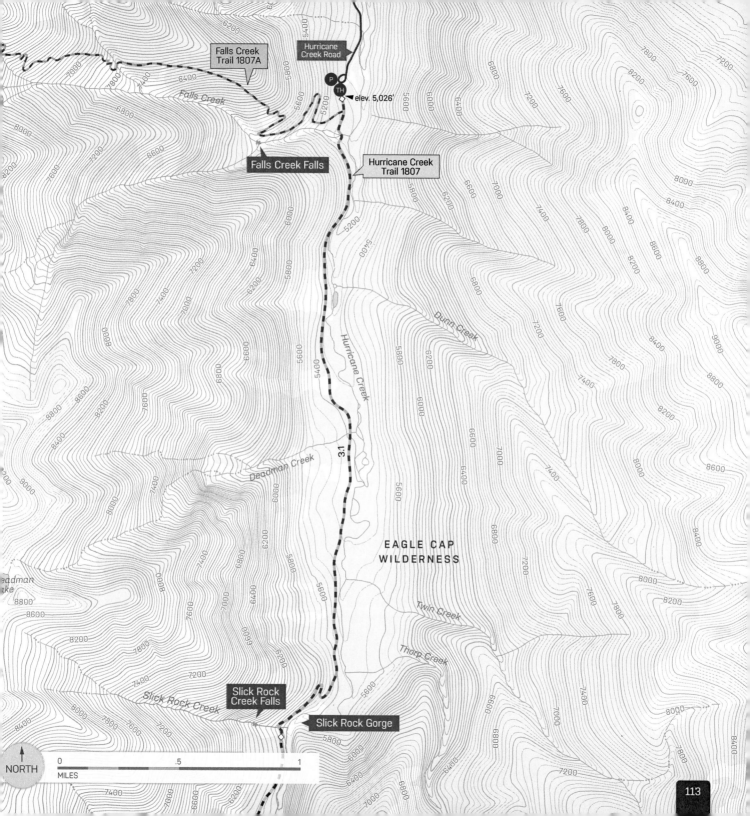

Falls Creek Trail 1807A

Hurricane Creek Road

Falls Creek

P TH
elev. 5,026'

Falls Creek Falls

Hurricane Creek Trail 1807

Dunn Creek

Hurricane Creek

3.1

Deadman Creek

EAGLE CAP
WILDERNESS

Twin Creek

Deadman Lake

Thorp Creek

Slick Rock Creek

Slick Rock Creek Falls

Slick Rock Gorge

NORTH

0   .5   1
MILES

Ride the Wallowa Lake Tramway 3,700 feet up to Mount Howard for spectacular panoramic views of the rugged Wallowa Mountains. A short trail loops around the summit of Mount Howard, with viewpoints in all directions.

Located just south of Wallowa Lake and the town of Joseph, Oregon, the Wallowa Lake Tramway takes riders from the Wallowa Lake Valley floor (4,550 ft.) to the summit of Mount Howard (8,150 ft.). Tickets for the tram cost $31 for adults, with discounts for seniors, students, and kids under 11 (2016 rates). The ride to the top takes about 15 minutes, exiting near the Summit Grill and Alpine Patio restaurant. Resist the tempation to feed the Columbia and golden-mantled ground squirrels, chipmunks, and Clark's nutcracker birds that frequently beg for food near the restaurant's patio. They are wild animals that are much better off when left to feed on the plentiful grasses and seeds located here.

For the loop hike, take the trail next to the patio and stay right at all junctions. Known as the High Wallowa Loop National Recreation Trail, this loop hike has five designated viewpoints, with interpretive signs about the area.

In just 1/8 of a mile, a short side trail leads to the Royal Purple viewpoint, with outstanding views of the jagged high peaks of the Wallowas. Continue on the loop to the Summit Overlook, Highlands Overlook and to the Snake River Country and Seven Devils viewpoint, with views towards Hells Canyon and Idaho. The Valley Overlook is perched high above the Wallowa Valley, including Wallowa Lake and the town of Joseph. A launch site for paragliding and hang gliding is located near the viewpoint. Continue on the loop trail to return to the tram terminal.

The alpine meadows on Mount Howard bloom in July and August, with several varieties of penstemon, red mountain heather, lance-leaf stonecrop, oval-leaf and alpine golden buckwheats, old man's whiskers, field locoweed, fleabane, and alpine goldenrod. Wallowa penstemon and Greenmann's desert parsley are rare plants found only in the Wallowa Mountains. Alpine wildflowers are easily damaged, so please stay on the trails to protect this fragile alpine environment.

The Nez Perce tribe lived in the Wallowa Valley for thousands of years before being expelled by General Howard (for whom this mountain is named) and his calvary. Chief Joseph led his people 1,500 miles before surrendering. His words still stir emotion about the wrongs committed to the native people during this time: "My heart is sick and sad. . . . From where the sun now stands, I shall fight no more forever." Visit the Wallowa Band Nez Perce Trail Interpretive Center in Joseph, Oregon to learn more about the customs and culture of the indigenous inhabitants.

Photos, left to right from top: panoramic view of the Wallowas from the Royal Purple Overlook; hang glider coming in for a landing; Mount Howard Tram; trail through evergreens; view to the north with Wallowa Lake and the Wallowa valley.

DISTANCE: 1.9 miles (roundtrip)
ELEVATION GAIN: 300 ft.
DIFFICULTY: easy
HIKE TYPE: loop (plus a tram ride)
TRAIL: dirt and rock
OPEN: late May - late Sept.
BEST TIME OF YEAR: July - August
FEATURES: panoramic views
FEES/PERMITS: fee to ride tram
AGENCY: Wallowa-Whitman National Forest

DIRECTIONS TO TRAILHEAD

From Portland, take I-84 East for 261 miles to Exit 261 Highway 82 / La Grande.

Turn right and continue on Highway 82, following signs for Wallowa Lake for 76 miles to the town of Joseph.

Continue through the town of Joseph and past Wallowa Lake to the parking area for the Wallowa Lake Tramway.

DRIVE TIME FROM PORTLAND
5 hours 50 minutes

MOUNT HOWARD

Photos, left to right from top: view to the east, towards Hells Canyon and Idaho; the tram ride up Mount Howard; one of many resident ground squirrels; the restaurant at the top of the tram; one of the trails at the top of Mount Howard.

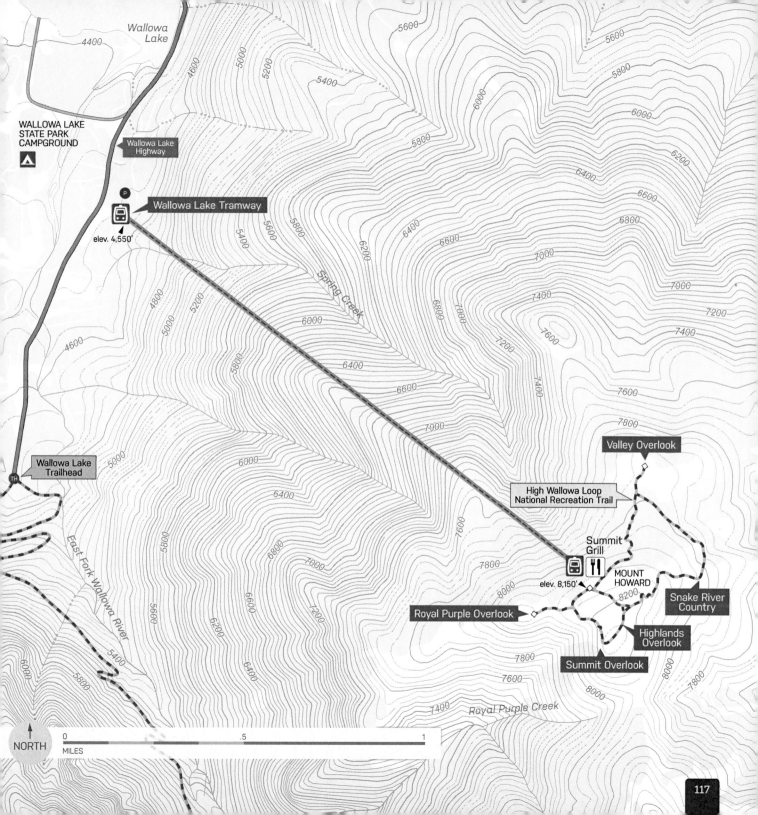

Wallowa Lake

WALLOWA LAKE
STATE PARK
CAMPGROUND

Wallowa Lake
Highway

Wallowa Lake Tramway
elev. 4,550'

4400

5600

5600

5800

6000

6200

6400

6600

6800

7000

7200

7400

Spring Creek

Wallowa Lake
Trailhead

East Fork Wallowa River

Valley Overlook

High Wallowa Loop
National Recreation Trail

Summit
Grill
elev. 8,150'

MOUNT
HOWARD

Snake River
Country

Royal Purple Overlook

Highlands
Overlook

Summit Overlook

Royal Purple Creek

NORTH

0   .5   1

MILES

117

Plan a three or four day backpacking trip to the popular Lake Basin area in the Wallowas and camp near Mirror Lake. Multiple options exist for longer hikes, including to the summit of Eagle Cap.

The Wallowas are better suited for backpacking than day hiking, primarily due to the distance required to reach the premier destinations in this mountain range.

The Two Pan trailhead (5,600 ft.) provides the best direct access into the Eagle Cap Wilderness, with the Lostine Canyon Road heading directly south from the small town of Lostine, Oregon for 18 miles to the edge of the Eagle Cap Wilderness. Fill out a free wilderness permit at the trailhead (groups are limited to 12, including dogs or stock animals, except in the Lakes Basin, where groups are limited to six). A small campground is located at the trailhead.

The use of pack animals such as horses and llamas is common in the Wallowas. When encountering them on the trail, move off to the downhill side if possible until they pass.

For a three-day trip, hike 7.5 miles to Mirror Lake, but for an easier backpacking trip, stay an extra night and camp in the Lostine Meadow area the first and last nights, with a recommended stay of two nights in the Lakes Basin. This area is very popular and can be crowded during the summer, so arriving mid-week is recommended.

From the trailhead, take the trail to a junction and stay left, taking the East Fork Lostine River Trail #1662. Cross the East Lostine River on a small bridge, and continue through a forest with Douglas fir, lodgepole pine, and spruce. The trail steepens and climbs 11 switchbacks over the next couple of miles. At three miles in, enter the Lostine Meadow area, with views of Eagle Cap in the distance. The meadows continue for about two miles, with several places to camp in treed areas next to the meadows. Cross a small bridge and then the trail leaves the meadows, climbing for two more miles to a trail junction near Mirror Lake. In the Lakes Basin, many areas to camp are dispersed throughout the granite-filled alpine area. Be sure to setup camp at least 100 feet away from the lakes, and plan to use a bear canister or hang your food to keep it safe. Campfires are strictly prohibited in the Lakes Basin.

Once in the Lakes Basin area, there are many choices of trails to explore. Eagle Cap (9,572 ft.) looms directly above. Take a trail all the way to the summit of this peak for outstanding views in all directions. Other trails in this area lead to a loop hike of the Lakes Basin; over Minam Pass to Minam Lake; or over Glacier Pass to Glacier Lake.

DISTANCE: 14.8 miles (roundtrip)

ELEVATION GAIN: 2,020 ft.

DIFFICULTY: moderate to difficult

HIKE TYPE: out and back, with loop options

TRAIL: dirt and rock, often dusty

OPEN: mid-July - Oct.

BEST TIME OF YEAR: mid-July - Aug.

FEATURES: subalpine meadows, alpine lakes, mountain views

FEES/PERMITS: Northwest Forest Pass required; self-issued wilderness permit

AGENCY: Wallowa-Whitman National Forest; Eagle Cap Wilderness

DIRECTIONS TO TRAILHEAD

From Portland, take I-84 East for 261 miles to Exit 261 Highway 82 / La Grande.

Turn right and continue on Highway 82, following signs for Wallowa Lake for 71.4 miles to Lostine River Road in the town of Lostine.

Turn right on Lostine River Road and continue for 18 miles to the trailhead.

DRIVE TIME FROM PORTLAND
5 hours 50 minutes

Photos, left to right from top: Eagle Cap and Mirror Lake; East Lostine River; Lostine Meadow with Eagle Cap in the distance.

LOSTINE MEADOW + MIRROR LAKE

Photos, left to right from top: view towards Mocassin Lake; Mirror Lake; Eagle Cap Wilderness sign; Two Pan Trailhead; creek from Mirror Lake to Mocassin Lake; enjoying the view of Eagle Cap and Mirror Lake.

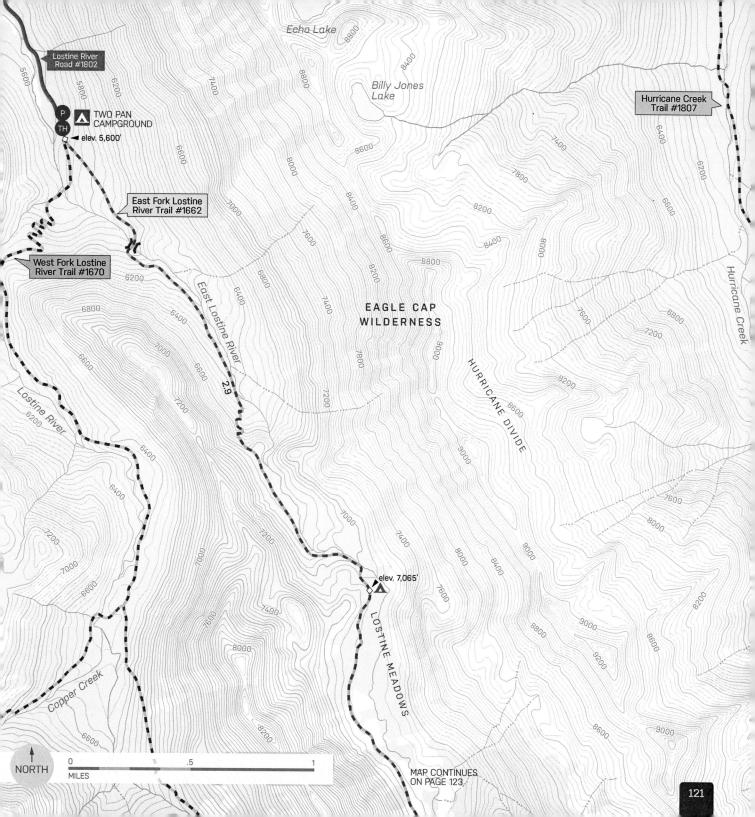

Echo Lake

Lostine River
Road #1802

Billy Jones
Lake

Hurricane Creek
Trail #1807

P
TH
elev. 5,600'

TWO PAN
CAMPGROUND

East Fork Lostine
River Trail #1662

West Fork Lostine
River Trail #1670

EAGLE CAP
WILDERNESS

East Lostine River

2.9

Lostine River

HURRICANE DIVIDE

Hurricane Creek

elev. 7,065'

Copper Creek

LOSTINE MEADOWS

NORTH

0   .5   1
MILES

MAP CONTINUES
ON PAGE 123

LOSTINE MEADOW + MIRROR LAKE

Photos, left to right from top: campsite at Mirror Lake; East Fork Lostine River Trail; Mirror Lake at sunset; "Eagle Cap" spelled out in rocks; trail; Mirror Lake and Eagle Cap at sunset.

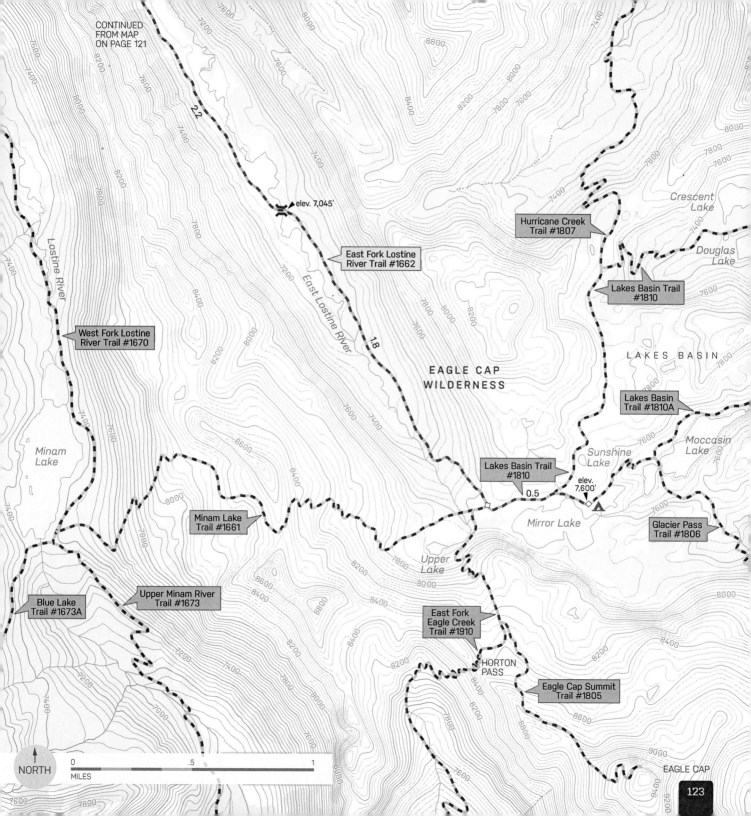

CONTINUED
FROM MAP
ON PAGE 121

2.2

elev. 7,045'

East Fork Lostine
River Trail #1662

Lostine River

East Lostine River

1.8

Hurricane Creek
Trail #1807

Crescent
Lake

Douglas
Lake

Lakes Basin Trail
#1810

West Fork Lostine
River Trail #1670

EAGLE CAP
WILDERNESS

LAKES BASIN

Lakes Basin
Trail #1810A

Moccasin
Lake

Minam
Lake

Sunshine
Lake

Lakes Basin Trail
#1810

elev.
7,600'

0.5

Minam Lake
Trail #1661

Mirror Lake

Glacier Pass
Trail #1806

Upper
Lake

Blue Lake
Trail #1673A

Upper Minam River
Trail #1673

East Fork
Eagle Creek
Trail #1910

HORTON
PASS

Eagle Cap Summit
Trail #1805

NORTH

0   .5   1
MILES

EAGLE CAP

123

Surrounded by granite peaks and subalpine meadows, the Lakes Basin in the Wallowas is a premier destination for mountain scenery while backpacking in the area.

A visit to the Lakes Basin is best done as a day hike while backpacking in the area, otherwise it's a very long day hike – 20 miles roundtrip with 2,770 ft. elevation gain if done from the Two Pan trailhead. However, if you are backpacking in the Lakes Basin area, it's an easy day hike.

Beginning at Mirror Lake, take the Lakes Basin Alternate Trail #1810A for a counter-clockwise loop through the Lakes Basin. On the way to Moccasin Lake, the trail loses about 120 feet of elevation. A trail junction with the Glacier Pass Trail leads over Glacier Pass to Glacier Lake. Pass this junction, continuing on the Lakes Basin trail to Moccasin Lake. Several side trails lead to good views of this lake, with views of the high ridge above.

Continue past Moccasin Lake to Douglas Lake, losing another 140 feet of elevation. A wide section of granite beside Douglas Lake makes for a great stop before continuing on the loop. At a trail junction at the end of Douglas Lake, turn left at the Lakes Basin Trail #1810. The trail travels along the north side of Douglas Lake, passing by tiny Craig Lake, then Crescent Lake. There are several nice campsites at the end of Douglas Lake.

Past Crescent Lake, the trail begins an ascent, with several switchbacks and 350 feet of elevation gain up to a junction with the Hurricane Creek Trail #1807. Stay to the left, continuing on the Lakes Basin Trail. Passing through several lovely meadow areas, after about a mile, arrive at Sunshine Lake, a smaller version of Mirror Lake, with great views of Eagle Cap. A short distance ahead, arrive back at Mirror Lake.

Campfires are strictly prohibited in the entire Lakes Basin, and campsites must be at least 100 feet from any lake. The entire area is filled with granite slabs, shelves, and walls, and views of Wallowa peaks loom in every direction. The Matterhorn and its 3,000 ft. face of white marble is visible from the section from the Hurricane Creek trail junction and Sunshine Lake.

NOTE: THIS IS DONE AS A DAY HIKE WHILE BACKPACKING IN THE LAKES BASIN

DISTANCE: 5.2 miles (roundtrip)

ELEVATION GAIN: 750 ft.

DIFFICULTY: easy to moderate

HIKE TYPE: loop

TRAIL: dusty dirt

OPEN: mid-July - Oct.

BEST TIME OF YEAR: mid-July - Aug.

FEATURES: subalpine meadows, mountain lakes, mountain views

FEES/PERMITS: Northwest Forest Pass required

AGENCY: Wallowa-Whitman National Forest; Eagle Cap Wilderness

DIRECTIONS TO TRAILHEAD

From Portland, take I-84 East for 261 miles to Exit 261 Highway 82 / La Grande.

Turn right and continue on Highway 82, following signs for Wallowa Lake for 71.4 miles to Lostine River Road in the town of Lostine.

Turn right on Lostine River Road and continue for 18 miles to the trailhead.

DRIVE TIME FROM PORTLAND
5 hours 50 minutes

Photos, left to right from top: Mocassin Lake; granite landscape; meadow and view of Eagle Cap.

LAKES BASIN

Photos, left to right from top: Sunshine Lake; rocky meadow; creek meandering through a small meadow; Hurricane Creek trail junction; waterfall; Douglas Lake.

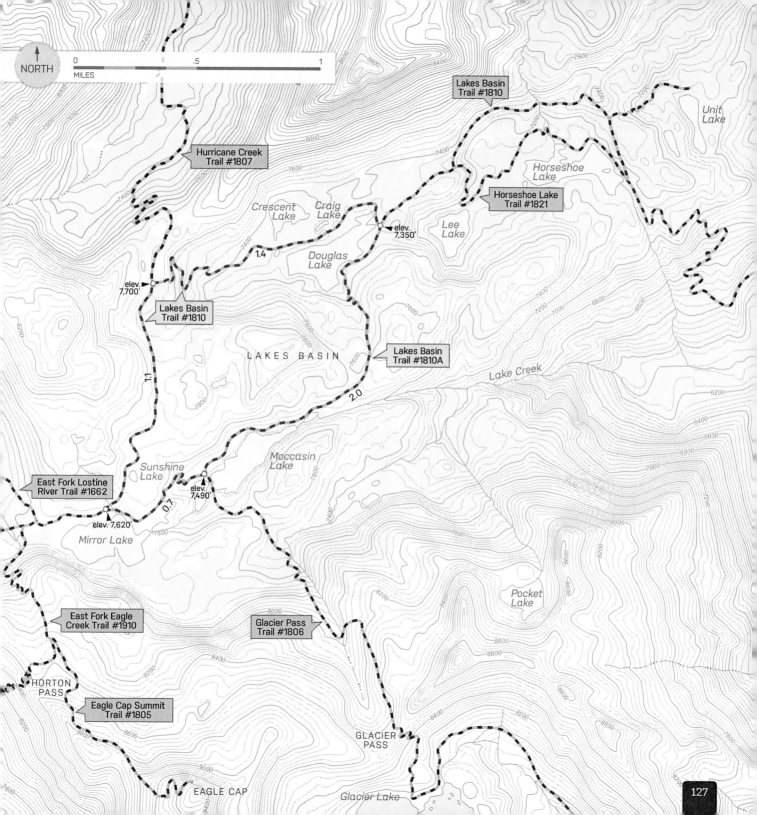

NORTH

MILES
0 .5 1

Lakes Basin
Trail #1810

Unit
Lake

Hurricane Creek
Trail #1807

Horseshoe
Lake

Horseshoe Lake
Trail #1821

Crescent
Lake

Craig
Lake

Lee
Lake

elev.
7,350'

1.4

Douglas
Lake

Lake Creek

elev.
7,700'

Lakes Basin
Trail #1810

LAKES BASIN

Lakes Basin
Trail #1810A

1.1

2.0

Sunshine
Lake

Moccasin
Lake

East Fork Lostine
River Trail #1662

elev.
7,490'

0.7

elev. 7,620'

Mirror Lake

Pocket
Lake

East Fork Eagle
Creek Trail #1910

Glacier Pass
Trail #1806

HORTON
PASS

Eagle Cap Summit
Trail #1805

GLACIER
PASS

EAGLE CAP

Glacier Lake

Hiking Resources

COLUMBIA RIVER GORGE

Columbia River Gorge National Scenic Area
fs.usda.gov/main/crgnsa

Friends of the Columbia Gorge
gorgefriends.org

CRATER LAKE

Crater Lake National Park
nps.gov/crla

Crater Lake Institute
craterlakeinstitute.com

Travel Southern Oregon
southernoregon.org

MOUNT HOOD

Mount Hood National Forest
fs.usda.gov/mthood

Mt Hood Cultural Center & Museum
mthoodmuseum.org

Timberline Lodge
timberlinelodge.com

OREGON COAST

Ecola State Park
bit.ly/ecolastatepark

Oregon Coast Tide Tables
or.usharbors.com/oregon-tide-charts

Oregon Coast Visitor Association
visittheoregoncoast.com

Oswald West State Park

bit.ly/oswaldwest

Samuel H. Boardman Scenic Corridor
bit.ly/samuelboardmancorridor

Siuslaw National Forest: Cape Perpetua Scenic Area
fs.usda.gov/siuslaw

PAINTED HILLS

John Day Fossil Beds National Monument
nps.gov/joda

SMITH ROCK

Smith Rock State Park
bit.ly/smithrockstatepark

SmithRock.com
smithrock.com

WALLOWAS

Wallowa-Whitman National Forest
fs.usda.gov/wallowa-whitman

Eagle Cap Wilderness
eaglecapwilderness.com

Joseph, Oregon
josephoregon.com

ENVIRONMENTAL ORGANIZATIONS

EarthShare Oregon
earthshare-oregon.org

Friends of the Columbia Gorge
gorgefriends.org

Oregon Sierra Club
oregon.sierraclub.org

Oregon Wild
oregonwild.org

GENERAL HIKING INFO

Ten Essentials
iheartpacificnorthwest.com/the-ten-essentials

Leave No Trace Principles
iheartpacificnorthwest.com/leave-no-trace

HIKING INFO & ORGANIZATIONS

Mazamas
mazamas.org

Oregon Hikers
oregonhikers.org

Outdoor Project
outdoorproject.com

Trailkeepers of Oregon
trailkeepersoforegon.org

Trails Club of Oregon
trailsclub.org

RECREATION PASSES

Northwest Forest Pass
discovernw.org

Oregon State Parks Pass
oregonstateparks.org

TOURISM

Travel Oregon
traveloregon.com

WEATHER CONDITIONS

NOAA
noaa.org

Oregon road conditions and webcams
tripcheck.com

Mountain Forecast
mountain-forecast.com

National Snow Analyses
nohrsc.noaa.gov/nsa

WILDFLOWERS

Oregon Wildflowers
oregonwildflowers.org

Wildflowers of the Pacific Northwest
pnwflowers.com

Index

About the Author

photo by Christine Taylor

Lisa D. Holmes

graphic designer, author, photographer

Hi! I'm Lisa Holmes, a graphic designer by trade and a hiking fanatic by accident. It is the combination of these two loves of mine that has enabled me to become a hiking book author as well.

Using the Bachelor of Fine Arts degree I earned at the Kansas City Art Institute, I've spent more than 25 years designing a successful career. But my life changed when I moved to Portland in 2007 and became obsessed with the beauty of the Pacific Northwest landscape.

I've since spent much of my time hiking the trails of Oregon and Washington and taking photographs of everything I've encountered. Combining my photos, my map and book design skills, and my desire to share my journey with others led me to the new career of creating books about the landscape I love.

In 2014, I began writing and designing a series of books to help others get out and discover the beauties of the Northwest landscape. *I Heart Oregon (& Washington): 25 of the Portland Area's Best Hikes* was the first in the series. And now I'm thrilled to introduce my second book, which features hike descriptions from each of Oregon's Seven Wonders.

Traveling and experiencing each of these amazing landscapes has been one of the most stimulating and satisfying endeavors I've ever undertaken.

So happy hiking! Be safe, always remember the ten essentials, and please treat the earth kindly.

Made in the USA
San Bernardino, CA
08 May 2016